Understanding SQL

Elizabeth Lynch

MACMILLAN

First published 1990

Published by
MACMILLAN EDUCATION LTD
Houndmills, Basingstoke, Hampshire RG21 2XS
and London
Companies and representatives
throughout the world

Typeset by
Ponting–Green Publishing Services, London

Printed in Great Britain by
Billing & Sons Ltd, Worcester

British Library Cataloguing in Publication Data
Lynch, E. (Elizabeth)
Understanding SQL. – (Macmillan computer science series).
1. Relational databases. Searching. Programming languages:
SQL
I. Title
005.756
ISBN 0–333–52433–0

Contents

Preface

This book is intended to be an introduction to the SQL database manipulation language. The coverage is not meant to be exhaustive; however, after reading the book you will have a good overall view of the concepts behind SQL and a working knowledge of its commands.

Although the book is based around the 1986 ANSI standard SQL, you will soon find out that no current SQL product implements the standard faithfully. We have tried to show you the ANSI commands, and in addition point out areas where some of the major SQL implementations differ (often for very good reasons) from the standard, and indeed, from each other.

We chose to use DB2, dBASE IV SQL, Informix and Professional Oracle as representatives of the wide range (over 50) of SQL implementations. DB2 is available on mainframes only; Informix and Oracle on mainframes, minis and Personal Computers (PCs), and dBASE IV SQL only on PCs. Throughout the text you will find ANSI SQL and these four SQLs used and contrasted in examples. Appendix B gives an overview of each product.

Chapter 12 gives a chart comparing their main features together with a brief guide to their divergences from the standard, any extra facilities they provide, and a general feel for what they are like to use.

However, this book is *not* intended to be a comprehensive guide to Oracle, dBASE, Informix and DB2! If you want to know more details about any particular SQL implementation, refer to its manuals, or to a book specifically about that SQL.

Note for dBASE (and other PC database system) users

Because SQL now comes 'packaged' with dBASE IV, many dBASE IV users will find themselves with a full-featured SQL system 'thrown in' with dBASE. In most cases, those users will have bought dBASE for the *dBASE* facilities, and not for the SQL features. If you are one of these people, you may well be wondering what SQL can do that dBASE cannot. Your situation is rather different from that of most other users of SQL databases, who have presumably chosen an SQL system for themselves on its own merits. We hope that this book will provide you with a introduction to SQL, and help you see how you might integrate SQL with dBASE IV.

If you have already been exposed to a non-SQL-based system, (for example, if you have previously used PC database systems such as dBASE or Paradox), you will naturally find yourself constantly comparing SQL to these, quite possibly initially to SQL's detriment. But you must realise that such comparisons are like comparing oranges to apples; both have their individual flavours and advantages, but are completely different. SQL and dBASE are alike only in that they both deal with data in a database system; as you will see, SQL is not a competitor to 'traditional' PC-based database systems, but will be used to *complement* them.

Acknowledgements

Many thanks are due to Oracle Corporation for providing the Oracle system on which the examples in this book were created and tested.

Thanks also to Paul, David, Andrew and Michael for encouraging me to write this book.

1 *Introduction to SQL*

Overview

In this chapter we will introduce you to SQL's history, to the **relational** concepts which gave birth to SQL, and to some of the reasons why SQL systems are to be preferred over 'traditional' database systems. Armed with this background information, you will be better equipped to begin looking at SQL commands in chapter 2.

1.1 A one-sentence definition of SQL

If we wanted to encapsulate all the important points about SQL in one sentence, the following statement would do the job quite well:

'SQL (pronounced 'Sequel' or 'Ess Cue Ell', and standing for 'Structured Query Language'), is a database language based on relational principles containing commands for manipulating data.'

The rest of this chapter is devoted to explaining what this really means!

1.2 A brief history of SQL

SQL was originally developed in the mid 1970s as an in-house research project by IBM, based on E.F. Codd's radically new way of describing data relationships – the **relational model**. (See section 1.3.4 and chapter 13 for more detail on what 'relational' means.) During this time, IBM published enough details of its work to allow other suppliers to develop SQL systems very similar to IBM's. The first commercial SQL systems were released in the late 1970s for use on IBM VM mainframes and Unix systems (Oracle, Ingres), shortly followed by IBM's SQL/DS for VM and VSE mainframe systems. In 1983 IBM released the SQL-based DB2 for the MVS operating system, and set the standard for mainframe database systems. Throughout the 1980s, database systems on mainframe and mini computers have been converging on relational, SQL-based systems.

1

Until recently, personal computers (PCs) have not been able to offer the computing power and fast disk access times necessary to run an SQL system efficiently. However, there are now many SQL systems available for PCs, including those which have 'migrated down' from Unix systems (Professional Oracle, Informix etc), and those which have been incorporated into existing PC database systems (dBASE IV SQL, R:base etc).

1.3 What SQL is and what it is not

Many people are confused about the role of SQL in the database world. If we look at what it is not, then it will be easier to clarify what SQL is.

It is *not*:

- a database management system (DBMS)
- a procedural programming language
- a fourth generation language (4GL)

It *is*:

- a powerful **data manipulation language** (DML) based on relational ideas
- a potential way to create portable database systems over hardware and software environments
- designed to be used both interactively, and embedded within procedural languages.

All this is explained in more detail below.

1.3.1 What is a database management system (DBMS)?

In a computer database system, all data is held in some physical form known as the 'database'. Access to the data is controlled by software known as the DBMS; it is the DBMS that 'knows' where and in what physical format the data is stored. The DBMS itself is accessed – for adding, updating, deleting and querying data – by a database language. SQL is an example of a database language; it is not itself a DBMS. The distinction between the 'database engine' provided by the DBMS, and the language used to 'drive' it, is an important one. In theory at least, the same DBMS could be accessed by different database languages, giving users flexibility in their choice of interface to data. However, in practice, you will find that for most purposes we can think of the DML and the DBMS as being synonymous.

So SQL is not a DBMS, but it is a database manipulation language.

1.3.2 *Programming languages, procedural languages, and 4GLs*

We said above that SQL is a database manipulation language (DML). Is it different from 'normal' computer languages such as BASIC and COBOL? The answer is a resounding 'Yes'. However, neither is it a Fourth Generation language. SQL's place in the scale of computer languages is explained below.

The main difference between a 'traditional' programming language such as COBOL, BASIC or C (also known as 'third generation languages'), and a 4GL, is that traditional languages are 'procedural'. In other words, a 4GL user simply tells the computer *what result is required* and the language itself works out how to achieve it; whereas a 3GL user has to specify to the computer exactly *how to obtain that result*. In an ideal world, all access to computer data would be undertaken through a 4GL; in practice, 3GLs still play a large part in most applications development.

Although SQL should certainly be grouped with the non-procedural languages (as you will see when looking at SQL commands in chapter 2), SQL is not itself a 4GL. One of the trademarks of a 4GL is that it provides a set of high-level tools in the form of screen and report designers, menu-creation utilities and so forth, relieving the user of the task of setting up such things himself. SQL itself has no such facilities. It provides neither 3GL programming constructs (loops, branches etc) nor 4GL user-friendly interfaces.

However, SQL is designed to be used, or 'embedded', within procedural programming languages (allowing users to use SQL's powerful data retrieval facilities in conjunction with any programmming tools required). Most buyers will also find that their implementation of SQL comes with 4GL-like facilities to make the use of SQL easier.

This does *not* mean that you can only use SQL from a 'high level' language. SQL commands can also be used interactively, with the user having direct access to the database. Indeed, this book concentrates almost exclusively on the 'interactive' use of SQL – after all, if you do not understand the basic SQL commands at their 'simplest' level, you will not get very far when trying to embed them in a host language! However, many potential users of SQL systems will find the SQL commands relatively difficult to learn, and will prefer to use 4GL form/report interfaces or to hire someone to write their SQL-based application for them in a 3GL/4GL.

It is this facility which allows existing PC database systems, such as dBASE IV, to accommodate SQL within their current command structures. The dBASE user can use SQL's data retrieval facilities to access data, and use dBASE itself as a programming language to do things with the data – such as display it in forms and reports.

The significance of SQL's position between the high-level 3GL and

4GLs, and the DBMS, is discussed in section 1.5 – 'The benefits of using SQL'.

1.3.3 *What is the relational model?*

We have mentioned that SQL is based on the principles of the relational database model first expounded by E.F. Codd (Codd 1970). But what does 'relational' mean?

Whole books have been devoted to just such a question. It is almost impossible to define relational meaningfully in a short paragraph, and we are not going to try! At this point, we will just describe some of the attributes of a relational system at an extremely superficial level, just so that you can have a 'feel' for what it is. In chapter 13 we discuss Codd's 'Fidelity Rules' for determining whether or not a system is relational in some detail, trying to translate them into layman's English rather than mathematical terms, and pointing out where SQL does or does not obey the rules.

You can certainly learn to use SQL efficiently even if you have no idea of its theoretical basis, just as you can drive a car well without knowing anything about mechanics. However, having a knowledge of relational theory, however slight, will help you see SQL in context, and give you a feel for probable developments in SQL.

So read chapter 13, either now or after you have learnt some SQL commands. If the only thing you learn from it is that SQL is *not* a fully relational DML, then you will have learned something extremely important!

1.3.4 *The relational model – a brief description*

As we said above, this section is not an attempt to summarise Codd's 12 rules (all of which any database system must implement to be called truly relational). Here we are merely giving a brief description of some of a relational system's trademarks.

The most obvious trademark of a relational database is that it holds data in **tables** consisting of **columns** and **rows**.

If you have used Paradox, dBASE IV in BROWSE mode, or even the Lotus 1–2–3 database (none of which is at all relational by Codd's rules) you have a good idea of the format of 'tabular' databases.

Here is a diagram of a typical table.

SURNAME	FIRSTNAME	ADDRESS	Q1TARGET
Smith	Susan	16, Fisher Close	15000
Robinson	John	3, Devon Gardens	70000
Adams	Evelyn	103, Mile End Rd.	50000

Rows are unordered when they are input. The data manipulation language (in our case, SQL) must provide a method for extracting subsets of columns and rows, and sequencing the rows in any desired order.

One of the features which, more than any other, marks a system as relational, is its ability to use a single command to extract information from several tables simultaneously. In SQL, this command is called SELECT. To take an example from the sales/order database which this book uses throughout for examples (see 2.4 for a full description), you could say:

```
SELECT surname, amount FROM salesmen,contracts
    WHERE salesmen.surname = contracts.surname;
```

to show all the value of each contract (from the contracts table) together with the name of the salesman responsible (from the salesmen table).

Columns can hold data of different types (e.g. Character, Number, Date). They can also hold a NULL value – meaning 'value unknown', (as distinct from 'blank' or 'zero'). Using NULLs is one example of the checks (or 'integrity constraints') that the DML has to provide to ensure that only correct data (relationally speaking) is allowed to be entered. For example, the relational model does not allow you to enter duplicate rows.

As you see from the above example, the user of a relational system does not need to know anything about file locations or physical data structures. Nor does he need to actively create links between tables (unlike dBASE IV's SET RELATION command). The DBMS is responsible for all the dirty work of keeping track of 'joining' tables to satisfy your queries. One of the tools that it uses to enable it to do this is the **System Catalog** – a record of all details about all tables in the database, which the DBMS is responsible for keeping updated. As a result, it should be possible to do things like move the database from one disk to another, and even redistribute it over different computers (e.g. on a network) without the user noticing that anything has changed.

1.3.5 *Implementations of the relational model*

There is no reason why there could not be several radically different DMLs from different suppliers implementing the relational model. But, in practice, the standard language that has emerged over the last 20 years is SQL. 'Standard', however, is a misnomer. There are more than 50 implementations of SQL currently available, none of which is identical with another or with any one standard!

Nor are any of the current SQLs fully relational. Codd bemoans the fact that even IBM's DB2 only 'scores' 7 out of 12 on the 12 Fidelity Rules.

So although relational theory has been accepted as being a sensible basis for data storage and access, we do not yet have a real relational system in the marketplace.

1.4 The 1986 ANSI Standard

A practical measurement of an SQL implementation is its conformity with the 1986 ANSI SQL standard. The ANSI standard is similar to IBM SQL, (which until then was the de facto standard), although it does contain several fairly important differences. You will find that most current SQL implementations will advertise themselves as conforming to either the IBM or the ANSI standard. Codd's associate Chris Date has published an interesting (and readable) book discussing the ANSI standard, its differences from DB2, and areas where he feels that better decisions could have been made as to what to include/exclude (Date 1988).

Since many current SQL implementations were in use well before the ANSI standard was published, there are several areas where, although the standard lays down sensible rules, virtually *none* of the major SQLs available today adheres to them! (A good example of this is the UNIQUEness concept discussed in 4.4.5.)

Similarly, there are areas where the ANSI standard seems to have deliberately ignored useful commands found in most SQLs anyway – for example, why does ANSI not provide a command to DROP (delete) a TABLE? And there are other areas where the ANSI SQL standard seems to deviate sharply from relational theory (for example in allowing duplicate rows).

So although the ANSI standard is a useful reference point by which to judge a particular SQL implementation, ANSI standard SQL is not necessarily the 'best' – that is, the most relational – SQL to adopt. To quote Codd himself (Codd, 1988)

'..DBMS vendors are rushing to support Structured Query Language (either IBM's version or its weaker ANSI cousin). This is like watching a flock of lemmings congregate on a beach in preparation for marching into the sea.'

Throughout this book we point out areas where the ANSI standard seems to be deficient, or diverges sharply from most actual implementations.

1.5 The benefits of using SQL

You may find it difficult to see just why SQL is so popular. Here are a few of the reasons which have contributed to its success.

a) A sound theoretical foundation

The relational model is generally accepted by experts as being a 'better' way of representing data structures. It is subject to stringent logical analysis, and every operation can be justified by the underlying mathematical theory.

b) IBM uses it

In the computer industry today, IBM's endorsement of any product is (usually) enough to guarantee its success. Once SQL/DS and DB2 became the IBM standard database systems, SQL's future was assured.

c) An SQL-based DBMS is flexible in terms of the languages, etc supported

In terms of controlling the database, SQL occupies a midway position between the 'high level' 4GL or 3GL language and the 'low level' DBMS software.

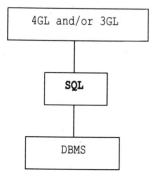

SQL's ability to act as a 'buffer' between the high-level programming languages and low-level DBMS software provides a clue to one of the reasons for its increasing popularity. For this 'midway' position offers the potential for different high-level and low-level components to be 'plugged in' around a standard SQL interface. In theory at least, future database users may be able to select both their preferred database engine and their interface to SQL. Suppliers of database systems are well aware of the possibilities offered by adopting the SQL standard.

d) *SQL-based systems are portable*

One of the big attractions of SQL is that it presents a standard interface for
data access across many different environments. Someone who learns SQL
on his dBASE IV PC could move to querying an IBM mainframe DB2
system with a minimum of retraining. In today's atmosphere of extending
distributed processing, this gives SQL a major advantage. Of course, this
argument only holds true so long as the user is happy to use 'core' SQL
commands. As mentioned above, once the SQL system is made 'user-
friendly' by the addition of 4GL tools such as menus, form designers and
report generators, the user becomes 'locked in' to that particular implementation. The interface to another implementation will be so different that
he might as well be learning a completely new package.

However, some SQL implementations are now available over different
hardware and software environments. Oracle, for example, is available for
PC-DOS systems, Unix and MVS. In addition, SQL servers for the PC are
now being released. An SQL server is a 'database' in the pure sense – that
is, an entity which holds data and which contains a set of commands to
query that data. It is not a programming language like dBASE. The database
may be accessed by any 4GL which knows the 'hooks' into the SQL server.

SQL systems will certainly continue to proliferate throughout the PC
world. As Unix becomes a more common choice for PC-based multi-user
systems, the databases of choice will all be SQL based (Informix, Oracle,
etc). IBM has included SQL as part of its Systems Applications Architecture
(SAA), which means that it has some commitment to continuing to offer
and develop SQL implementations; OS/2 Extended Edition contains an
implementation of SQL; and there are various third-party SQL servers
announced for OS/2 (for example, the Ashton-Tate/Microsoft collabora-
tion).

Summary

This chapter introduced you to SQL by explaining briefly its role in the
database world. You learnt *what* inspired its development (Codd's relational
model); *how* it proliferated through the computing community (minis,
mainframes, and then PCs), and *why* users might prefer SQL systems to
other databases (SQL is an IBM-endorsed standard which provides a powerful
DML that can be used as a front or back end to DBMSs and/or 4GLs).

In chapter 2 we will start to look at some of the 'jargon' terms that you
need to know in order to get on with learning the SQL commands.

2 SQL basic terms

Overview

This chapter explains some of the terminology used in an SQL system, the basic structure of SQL commands, and the syntax formats used by the commands.

2.1 Introduction

The aim of this chapter is to introduce you to the SQL terms that you need in order to be able to 'get going' with SQL. Other concepts and terms will be introduced as necessary in later chapters.

In this chapter we also introduce the sample database which will be used throughout the book for examples.

2.2 Databases

The term 'database' refers to the total collection of data concerning one particular topic. One computer system may hold many databases. Thus a typical business may have separate databases for:

- customers and invoices
- personnel details
- office equipment maintenance schedules
- individuals' personal telephone directories
- company car details

and so on.

Of course, deciding what items of data should logically be placed in the same database is a job for whoever designs the computerised database system. Some applications will require only one database; others will be more logically split into several. This book does not attempt to deal with the problems of database design (although chapter 3 does show SQL being used in the 'real life' development of a system); however, just using SQL databases will give you a feel for the correct structuring of data. There is no absolute 'right' or 'wrong' in database design; everything depends on the particular application's requirements. In the above example, separate databases may indeed be the best way to structure the data; however, you might also argue that office equipment and company cars should be 'linked' to the person who uses them; and that individual telephone lists will overlap, not only with each other but also with the main customer file. In this case, maybe a single database (although with separate tables – see below) will reflect the company's needs better.

Most SQL implementations have a command for creating an 'empty' database which can then be 'filled' with the tables which contain the actual data.

2.3 The example database used in this book

This book uses a salesmen/contracts database to illustrate all the SQL commands discussed in later chapters. It holds three tables; 'salesmen', 'contracts' and 'customers'. In chapter 3 you will see the rationale behind the building of this database and the separation of the data into different tables. Here we simply introduce the database to you so that you can make sense of the examples given later in this chapter.

The purpose of the database is to enable managers to track the performance of salesmen by seeing how the value of the contracts that they have won measures up against the quarterly targets set for them. Managers should also be able to see the value of orders placed by customers.

The 'Salesmen' table contains details of each salesman's 'personal' details, such as his employee number, first name, surname, address, phone number, and the quarterly target figures.

The 'Contracts' table holds details of every contract, including the name of the salesman who took the contract, the customer name, the value of the contract and the contract date.

The 'Customer' table holds the customer's 'personal' details, such as customer number, name, address, phone number etc.

2.4 Tables, rows and columns

In a relational database system, all the data is held in **tables**. A table is made up of **rows** and **columns**. These correspond to the **records** and **fields** in a traditional database system. The number of columns and rows allowed in a single table varies in different implementations of SQL.

You will also come across the terms 'base table' (one containing 'real' data where the data has physically been typed in) and 'result table' (the 'temporary' table created when a SELECT query is performed). Result tables are not available for further querying, although some SQLs provide a command to allow them to be 'converted' into base tables.

Sometimes you will find tables referred to as **relations**. This is common practice in discussions of the subject by relational database experts; most user guides and introductory level books stick to 'table'.

Example Table

SURNAME	FIRSTNAME	ADDRESS	Q1TARGET
Smith	Susan	16, Fisher Close	15000
Robinson	John	3, Devon Gardens	70000
Adams	Evelyn	103, Mile End Rd.	50000

The SQL SELECT command allows tables to be joined together so that information may be extracted from more than one table simultaneously.

2.5 Indexes

SQL allows you to set up **indexes** on tables to speed up data retrieval. An SQL index works in the same way as an index in a book, allowing you to 'look up' an entry immediately rather than having to scan the entire volume (table) to find what you are interested in. You can think of an index as a separate file containing a list of 'pointers' to the real data in the table.

Table	*Index*
Smith	1.Adams
Robinson	2.Robinson
Adams	3.Smith

Once indexes have been created on a table, SQL will automatically determine which, if any, of the possible indexes should be used for any particular query on the database.

Although you do not have to create any indexes at all, in most cases your system will perform more efficiently if each table is indexed on at least the primary key (see 2.6).

Indexes are discussed fully in chapter 9.

2.6 Primary and foreign keys

Each row should have a column or combination of columns, the contents of which distinguishes that row from all others. In other words, each row should be unique. The columns which make the row unique are together called the primary key of a table. (In practice, most SQL implementations, including the ANSI standard, do not actually *enforce* the use of primary keys, making it possible to have duplicate rows in a table.)

If a column which is a primary key in one table is reproduced in another table (not as the primary key of that table), then it is known as a **foreign key** on the second table.

2.7 SQL commands

SQL has about 30 commands which are used to manipulate the database system. To make it easier to remember them, they can be divided into three groups:

Data Definition commands   (e.g. CREATE TABLE)
Data Manipulation commands (e.g. SELECT, UPDATE)
Data Control commands   (e.g. COMMIT, ROLLBACK)

The precise number of commands will vary between SQL implementations. The area with the greatest variation in number and format of commands is that of Data Definition.

Appendix A gives a list of the ANSI SQL commands by category, together with a brief description of their function.

2.8 Entering an SQL statement

An SQL **statement** consists of the SQL command followed by any other mandatory or optional clauses necessary to complete a valid SQL operation. For example, the SQL command SELECT (used to extract rows and columns from one or more tables) becomes a statement like:

```
SELECT surname FROM salesmen;
```

Words like SELECT and FROM are known as **reserved words**. This means that you cannot give their name to data structures such as tables or columns. Most SQL implementations have about 150 reserved words.

All reserved words must be separated from the following word or data item name by at least one space. Thus

```
SELECT * FROM salesmen;
```

is legal, whereas

```
SELECT* FROM salesmen;
```

is not.

However, in some parts of statements, spaces are unimportant. For example, SQL would be equally happy to accept:

```
SELECT surname FROM salesmen WHERE surname='Smith';
```

and

```
SELECT surname FROM salesmen WHERE surname   =   'Smith';
```

or

```
SELECT surname,empno,q1target FROM salesmen;
```

and

```
SELECT surname,    empno  ,  target   FROM salesmen;
```

SQL commands usually have several parameters or optional clauses attached to them. This means that a single statement can end up being quite long. For example, the SELECT command has six different options (and even more in some implementations), a combination of some or all of which can be used to refine the exact data retrieved from the tables.

To make such statements clearer to understand, you can divide them over several lines when you type them in. For example:

```
SELECT
    salesmen.surname,
    salesmen.empno,
        contracts.amount,
    contracts.cdate
    FROM salesmen,contracts
        WHERE salesmen.empno = contracts.empno
        AND contracts.amount > 300000
    ORDER BY salesmen.surname;
```

You can divide up the statement into separate lines at whatever points you like, although it is conventional – and clear – simply to put separate clauses on different lines as in the above example. You can indent lines to make the structure of the statement easier to follow – SQL will just ignore superfluous spaces.

Some parameters to the command are mandatory; others are genuinely optional. In the SELECT example above, the only mandatory requirement is that one or more column names, and the tables to be queried, should be specified; the WHERE and ORDER BY clauses are options.

2.8.1 *Upper or lower case?*

In most implementations of SQL, you can type commands and field names in either upper case, lower case, or a mixture of both. Thus Oracle, for example, will be equally happy to accept (and produce the same result for):

```
SELECT amount FROM contracts;
```

and

```
Select AMOUNT from CONTRACTS;
```

However, Informix requires that all command words be in lower case, and would reject both the above examples in favour of:

```
select AMOUNT from CONTRACTS;
```

or

```
select amount from contracts;
```

In this book we show SQL commands in upper case characters to set them off from the rest of the text. Column and table names are shown in lower case.

The only time when upper/lower case can make a difference to the result of a query is when you specify the data you want to retrieve. Thus:

```
SELECT firstname,surname FROM salesmen
    WHERE surname = 'Smith';
```

will produce a different result table from

```
SELECT firstname,surname FROM salesmen
    WHERE surname = 'SMITH';
```

2.8.2 *Punctuation*

As you can see, the commands are English-like words. You will also come across the full-stop . , the comma ,, the semi-colon ;, and the quote mark '.

The semi-colon is used in many SQL implementations to indicate the end of an SQL statement:

```
SELECT surname FROM salesmen;
```

Not all implementations *require* a semi-colon at the end of a command line; however, nearly all will accept one if you enter it. This book always uses the semi-colon to indicate the end of a statement.

The comma separates lists of column names. For example:

```
SELECT surname,address,qltarget FROM salesmen;
```

The full stop separates table and column names. In a situation where you are extracting data from two tables at once and where a column with the same name appears in both tables, you will have to specify which table you want to pick up the column details from. For example:

```
SELECT salesmen.surname,contracts.amount,contracts.surname
    FROM salesmen,contracts;
```

The quote mark encloses all information of data type **character**. (See chapter 4 for a discussion of SQL data types.) Thus

```
SELECT firstname,surname FROM salesmen
    WHERE surname = 'Smith';
```

Leaving out the quotes will produce an error message.

Summary

In this chapter you learned the basic terminology and rules about SQL usage that you will need for understanding the SQL commands.

In the next chapter we will look at a 'real life' example of how an SQL system might be created, used, and changed to reflect the users' changing needs.

3 An example of setting up an SQL system

Overview

This chapter shows SQL being used for 'real-life' development of a database system.

We introduce some of the common SQL commands, and see how they can flexibly change the database as the user's ideas develop.

Major commands mentioned in this chapter

CREATE TABLE   INSERT VALUES
SELECT   CREATE VIEW
GRANT   REVOKE
CREATE INDEX

3.1 Introduction

Before we start to examine the SQL commands in detail over the next few chapters, it will be useful for you to have a feel for how SQL is actually used in database design.

This chapter shows how SQL might be used in a real-life development of a system. We will see how SQL can cope easily with supporting the users 'mistakes' in data design – mistakes which nevertheless reflect the way that the user actually perceives and works with his data, as opposed to the 'false' way in which the data has to be organised on the computer system. SQL will eventually persuade the user to adopt efficient data structures, while continuing to allow him to access and view the data in the ways which to him seem most sensible.

This chapter will also introduce you to some of the basic SQL commands so that you can get an 'instant appreciation' of what is involved in setting up an SQL database.

In the examples given below, no attempt is made to explain fully the workings of the SQL commands used. We have given a general explanation of the function of the command where necessary, and have indicated where the command can be found covered in greater depth elsewhere in the book. The aim of this chapter is to give you a feeling for the power and scope of SQL, not an in-depth syntax guide.

You will also see that we make no attempt to cover *all* the commands that would inevitably be involved in setting up a real system.

In fact, as you will see, most of the example revolves around the SELECT command – the one that allows users to retrieve specified rows and columns from existing tables.

3.2 Designing a database

The goal of anyone setting up a database system must be to design a system which reflects the real-world use of data as closely as possible. Different users will have different uses for the same data; some users do not need to see some parts of the database, and so on. So the system needs to provide various **views** of the data. Associated with this is the need to provide database security, both in the sense of only permitting authorised users to access particular data, and in dealing correctly with transactions which are abandoned in mid-stream. Who wants a half-updated database? Yet another vital consideration is that no data should be duplicated around the database. Consider the disastrous confusion that would arise if the price of your company's major product appeared as £200 in the stock table, but as £100 in the invoice file.

Of course, in an ideal world, the database system would be perfectly planned before the developer ever touched a keyboard. But in the real world, such perfection rarely occurs. This is especially true now that SQL has migrated to the PC world, where the traditional approach of users accustomed to relatively easy-to-use, menu-driven, help-filled applications, tends to be to jump in and write the system first, and iron out the kinks later.

SQL has no magic formulas for enforcing 'good' design. But it does have flexibility which allows users to develop systems 'on the fly', and then to tune them afterwards; it does provide satisfactory methods of controlling security; and it does provide **integrity constraints** which can help to ensure that problems such as unnecessary duplication of data will not occur.

If we follow through an example of a 'typical' user's progress in developing a system to reflect accurately his real-life data and needs, we will see that SQL provides a very adaptable tool for doing it.

3.3 Using SQL to create a database

3.3.1 The example system

Let us take a system that tracks a salesman's performance against a target. The user has to keep data on each salesman as follows:

- – 'personal' details (name, employee number, address etc)
- – quarterly targets
- – contracts won (customer name, address, amount, date etc)

He will need to extract information both by salesman and by customer to see reports on, among other things,

- – all salesmen's target figures
- – salesman's performance against target
- – total orders placed by any one customer

3.3.2 The 'first stab' table

Most users do not automatically consider the data from which they run their business as lending itself easily to being split up into different units – or **tables**. They view the data which is important to tham as a logical whole. Most first-time users of relational database systems will attempt to put *all* data into one large table. For example, the initial reaction of the user of the sales system might be to use CREATE TABLE to set up a table with the following columns (holding each salesman's 'personal' details, their quarterly targets, and the customer details for every contract that the salesman makes):

Creating a table

```
CREATE TABLE salesmen
      (surname    char(20);
      firstname   char(15),
      empno       char(5) NOT NULL,
      address     char(30),
      telephone   char(12),
      q1target    number(6),
      q2target    number(6),
      q3target    number(6),
      q4target    number(6),
      c1custname  char(30),
      c1custadd   char(30),
      c1amount    number(6),
```

```
c1date      date,
c2custname  char(30),
c2custadd   char(30),
c2amount    number(6),
c2date      date,
c3custname... )
etc..
```

(specifying that the employee number be NOT NULL means that a value *must* be entered for this column).

The structure looks, and is, long and unwieldy – and, as you will soon see, it is certainly not the most efficient way to hold the contract data.

However, the user can certainly perform other essential operations on the table, such as entering new rows, selecting a set of rows for display, and deleting and updating rows. Here are examples of all these operations.

Inputting a row of data – INSERT VALUES

```
INSERT INTO salesmen VALUES
    ('Smith',
    'John',
    '10001',
    '16, Mayfly Close, London',
    '01-987-6543',
    50000,
    50000,
    75000,
    100000,
    'Jones Bros.',
    '99, The High Rd., Salisbury',
    15000,
    TO_DATE('7-AUG-90'),
    'Brown & Co.',
    'Unit 1, Trading Estate',
    7000,
    TO_DATE('25-SEP-90');
```

(to add a row for John Smith and the two contracts that he has won so far this year).

A simple SELECT query to retrieve data

```
SELECT surname,qltarget
  FROM salesmen
    WHERE qltarget > 100000
  ORDER BY surname;
```

(to view the names and targets of salesmen whose target figure is greater than 100000, sequenced in alphabetical order by salesman's surname).

Deleting a row – DELETE

```
DELETE FROM salesmen
    WHERE empno = '10001';
```

(to delete the row for employee number 10001).

Updating rows – UPDATE

```
UPDATE salesmen
    SET qltarget = qltarget*2;
```

(to double everyone's Quarter 1 target).

Problems with this structure

However, the user will realise very quickly that cramming all fields into one table is going to force him to duplicate data items which should only be in the system once (for example, customer names etc), and will completely preclude him from making some of the queries that he needs to be able to perform. He will have to impose artificial restrictions on the data; for example, he will have to decide on the maximum number of contracts that a salesman will take. Using the table structure given above, he cannot store contract details efficiently; for each new contract he will have to create new columns in the database. If an exceptionally successful salesman makes 100 sales in the year, then the table will not only be unwieldy and confusing to view, but will break the 'number of columns' limit in several SQL implementations! And the table will contain large numbers of columns that will, for many rows, be left empty. On any SQL implementation using fixed length fields this will waste disk space; in any case, the table will be incredibly unwieldy to use.

To see the salesman's performance for Quarter 1, the user would have to give the command

```
SELECT c1amount + c2amount + c3amount + c4amount ..
(up to the maximum number of contract columns he
had to set up in the table)..
       FROM salesmen
       WHERE surname = 'Smith'
             AND contdate < TO_DATE('01-APR-90');
```

As you can see, in practice this table structure would be unusable.

3.3.3 *Reorganising the table – 1. Removing duplicate columns*

Perhaps his first thought might be to add extra contracts by row rather than by column. He might redesign the database (by CREATING a new table with the columns he requires, doing multiple SELECTs to extract each set of contract data to a TEMPorary table, and using INSERT INTO..SELECT.. to transfer the TEMP tables to the new table) to have the following columns:

```
CREATE TABLE salesmen
       (surname    char(20),
        firstname  char(15),
        empno      char(5) NOT NULL,
        address    char(30),
        telephone  char(12),
        q1target   number(6),
        q2target   number(6),
        q3target   number(6),
        q4target   number(6),
        custname   char(25),
        custadd    char(30),
        amount     number(6),
        contdate   date);
```

and enter *one row for each contract*. This now lets him show all contracts for one salesman with:

```
SELECT custname,amount,contdate
    FROM salesmen
       WHERE surname = 'Smith';
```

He can even get a 'Quarter 1 performance against target' summarised report from the table showing one line for every salesman with his name and the total value of all his contracts for the first three months of the year:

```
SELECT surname,qltarget,sum(amount) FROM salesmen
    WHERE contdate < TO_DATE('1-Apr-90')
    GROUP BY surname;
```

And since only one customer is shown in any one row, he could get a list of all current customers with:

```
SELECT DISTINCT custname FROM salesmen;
```

However, the problem of data duplication is still there, since the salesman's name, targets, etc have to be repeated in every row. Obviously, this structure is not the correct solution.

3.3.4 Reorganising the database – 2. Creating separate tables

At this stage the SQL user has to be told that the correct way to store this data is in several separate tables. This system would probably need tables for:

1. Salesman's main details (Salesman's name, employee number, address, phone, targets etc)
2. Customer main details (Customer name, address, phone etc)
3. Contract details (Customer name, contract number, contract date, amount, employee number of salesman responsible)

Since enquiries will need to access data from several tables simultaneously, the user will have to designate one column in his tables as being a 'link' between tables. For example, in order for SQL to be able to perform a query showing the salesman's name (from the 'salesmen' table) and a list of all his contracts (from the 'contract' table), the two tables must have some column value in common. In our example, the employee number appears in both tables, providing a cross-reference by which SQL can extract the correct rows.

Having set up these three tables, the SELECT command to extract the required data for reports is hardly more complicated than the examples above. To generate the 'performance against target' report, you would say:

```
SELECT surname,qltarget,sum(amount)
    FROM salesmen,contracts
    WHERE salesmen.empno = contracts.empno
        AND contdate < TO_DATE('1-APR-90')
    GROUP BY surname;
```

The data integrity of the system is easy to preserve, since now the 'personal' details for each salesman and customer are only held once.

Is this more complicated to use?

Although the table structure has now been improved – or 'normalised', the user has now apparently lost the ability to view his data as a whole. Whatever the shortcomings of his original attempt at setting up a single table holding all possible data items, he could at least see all relevant columns at a single glance. Saying

```
SELECT * FROM salesmen
        WHERE surname = 'Smith'
        AND firstname = 'John';
```

then showed him absolutely everything about John Smith's current 'personal' and 'contract' state. Now that the data is divided over three tables, he apparently has to issue an SQL statement like

```
SELECT * FROM salesmen,contracts,customers
        WHERE salesmen.surname = 'Smith'
        AND salesmen.firstname = 'John'
        AND salesmen.empno = contracts.empno
        AND customers.custname = contracts.custname;
```

every time he wants to see these details. But in fact, if such joining together of data is a common occurrence, the user can create a **view** of the data to show exactly the columns he requires.

3.3.5 *Reorganising the database – 3. Creating a VIEW*

Views are an exceptionally important feature of SQL in that they allow users to look at – or 'view' – data at a level once removed from the 'real' underlying tables. Views appear to the user to be 'real' tables; however, they are in fact 'result' tables created as a result of a 'formula' – or SELECT statement. A full discussion of views is given in chapter 8, and we will not go into their setup in detail here. Suffice it to say that, by giving the command:

```
CREATE VIEW salesview AS
        SELECT * FROM salesmen,contracts,customers
        WHERE salesmen.surname = 'Smith'
        AND salesmen.firstname = 'John'
        AND salesmen.empno = contracts.empno
        AND customers.custname = contracts.custname;
```

the user will create a permanent view of the database which will allow him to look at John Smith's details at any time just by saying:

```
SELECT * FROM salesview;
```

So the user has kept the ability to access his data as *he* wants – as one logical whole – while being forced by SQL to structure the underlying tables in a way which preserves the data integrity of the system.

3.3.6 Security – views and privileges

The very fact that different views of the database can be created for different users provides a simple way of restricting data access. The managing director can be told to use the view permitting him to see all aspects of salesmen's performance; the accounts clerk can be told the name of the view which only shows customers' invoice details.

However, normally you must rely on more than just users' goodwill to stop them using tables which they are not supposed to see! SQL provides the GRANT command to allow users to be granted different 'privilege levels' of access; to the database, to base tables and to views. This is one of the areas where the various SQL implementations differ in the privileges allowed and the precise form of the command. Using Oracle, the user could say

```
GRANT connect TO liz IDENTIFIED BY mypass;
```

to allow the user 'liz' to **log on** to Oracle only when she enters the password 'mypass'.

```
GRANT update ON salesview TO liz;
```

will allow 'liz' to **make changes** to the data shown in the view 'salesview'. But

```
GRANT select ON salesview TO liz;
```

will only let her **query** the data in 'salesview'.

The REVOKE command is used to remove privileges once GRANTed.

3.3.7 Security – COMMIT and ROLLBACK

SQL gives you the chance to change your mind about whether changes to the database are correct or not. In an SQL system, no changes to data are permanent until the user issues the command

```
COMMIT WORK;
```

If you add a row to a table, and then query the database, your new row will appear in the result table. But it is not *really* in the base table yet. You can stop it ever having a place in the base table, with the command

```
ROLLBACK;
```

So, provided that the user has the sense not to COMMIT when not appropriate, it is always possible to revert to a previous version of the database. (Since you probably cannot trust the user always to display such good sense, a practical SQL application may need to use the SQL commands 'embedded' within a programming language or 4GL which can be relied upon to COMMIT or ROLLBACK at an appropriate time.)

Many SQL implementations have a command such as Oracle's

```
SET AUTOCOMMIT ON;
```

which will automatically commit work after each transaction. This is especially useful when you are using SQL 'interactively'.

3.3.8 Integrity constraints

SQL has several commands which can be used to stop users from entering 'incorrect' data. For example, to go some way towards avoiding the 'data duplication' problem mentioned in section 3.1, we could have specified the NOT NULL UNIQUE option on the employee number column in the 'salesmen' table:

```
CREATE TABLE salesmen
        (empno   (char 5) NOT NULL UNIQUE,
        surname (char 20),
        etc ...
```

The system would then not allow the entry of two employees with the same employee number. (Another way of achieving the same result is to CREATE a UNIQUE INDEX on this column.) And some SQL implementations will automatically reject duplicate rows.

Summary

This chapter showed you how SQL combines power and flexibility to allow databases not only to contain efficiently structured data, but also to reflect the database users' view of their data. To be able to combine the two viewpoints in one set of similar data structures is quite an achievement!

You also met essential SQL commands allowing you to create a table, input data, perform simple queries on one or more tables, create and use views, and grant access privileges to tables. All these commands will be given greater coverage in the following chapters.

In chapter 4 we will start to examine SQL commands in detail, beginning with creating tables and inputting data.

4 Creating Databases and Tables Inputting Data

Overview

In this chapter we show you how to start and finish an SQL session, set up new tables, alter the columns a table contains, type in rows of data, and get rid of a table altogether.

A full discussion of the various methods of inputting, updating and deleting rows is given in chapter 7. This chapter just shows you the simplest way to enter a row of data.

We will also discuss how various implementations set up, use and delete databases, and how Data Dictionary information is kept in the System Catalog.

Major commands covered in this chapter

CREATE TABLE	CREATE DATABASE
ALTER TABLE	START DATABASE
DROP TABLE	DROP DATABASE
INSERT VALUES	QUIT/EXIT

4.1 Starting and finishing an SQL session

4.1.1 Starting an SQL session

Before you can start creating databases and tables, you have to know how to start an SQL session – or 'log on' to SQL. The precise format of moving from your computer's operating system to the SQL product will vary slightly between implementations; however, most SQLs require you to:

1. Enter your 'user name'
2. Enter your password

These will have been assigned to you by the Database Administrator using SQL's GRANT command (see chapter 11 for details).

For example, to enter Oracle you would type:

```
SQLPLUS  liz/lizpass
```

to tell Oracle that the user called 'liz' wants to log in with the password 'lizpass'.

Once SQL has checked your entries as being valid, the SQL session will begin.

Note that dBASE IV SQL is unusual in that you first start a dBASE session (usually with no log-in procedures) and then start SQL from within dBASE with the command SET SQL ON.

4.1.2 Ending an SQL session

Most SQLs accept either:

```
QUIT
```

or

```
EXIT
```

to end the SQL session and return to the operating system.

Any tables still open will automatically be closed. Any work not yet COMMITted to the permanent database (see chapter 8) will be saved.

4.1.3 Suspending an SQL session

Some SQLs have a command which temporarily 'suspends' the SQL session and returns you to the operating system. Oracle uses '$' for this; dBASE IV SQL achieves nearly the same thing with the RUN command. This allows you to carry out short tasks at operating system level, and then return (using a command like Oracle's EXIT) to the SQL session, 'picking up' the session in exactly the same state as you left it.

4.2 Databases

4.2.1 What is a database?

As we gave the definition in the chapter 3, a database is a collection of data which can, and *should,* logically be grouped together. In practice, a database contains one or more SQL tables. There may be more than one database available on the same computer environment.

4.2.2 *Creating and using a database*

Note that the specification of databases is not defined by the ANSI standard, so you will find different commands and ways of implementing the concept over various different SQL implementations.

Most SQL implementations do provide a method of creating databases; unfortunately, the commands vary considerably both in syntax and scope over different implementations. Here we will just introduce some of the common forms under which this facility is found; you will have to check the documentation of any particular implementation to find out the exact form of its 'database' facility.

Sometimes the command is included within the SQL command set (as in dBASE IV SQL), in other cases there is a separate utility 'create' program which runs at the operating system level to create a 'databasespace' (as in DB2).

The most common forms under which this command is found are

```
CREATE DATABASE dbname;   (e.g. dBASE IV SQL, Informix)
```

and

```
CREATE SCHEMA dbname;     (ANSI standard)
```

Other implementations contain commands to group existing tables together for optimal performance – for example, Oracle's

```
CREATE CLUSTER clustername;
```

As a result of issuing such a command, disk storage space is allocated to this particular database in a way peculiar to the computer environment on which the implementation is running. dBASE IV SQL, for example, creates a new MS-DOS subdirectory for each database, and puts a separate copy of the system catalog tables into it to hold the data dictionary information for this database. (The System Catalog in discussed in section 4.3.)

Such a facility may exist on your system as being either mandatory or optional. If your SQL implementation demands this first step in database setup, then each time you want to access data you will have to tell the system which database to use, with a command like:

```
START DATABASE dbname;    (dBASE)
```

or

```
INVOKE dbname    (Informix)
```

There will almost certainly be a command such as

```
SHOW DATABASES;
```

to see a list of existing database names.

To remove a database from the system, use

```
DROP DATABASE dbname;
```

Be very careful when doing this, since DROPping a database will remove all its tables, views and indexes from the system forever!

4.3 The System Catalog

All information about existing databases (if appropriate), tables, indexes and views etc is stored in a special set of tables often referred to collectively as the System Catalog.

These tables store information such as:

- data table names
- table creators
- authorised users of tables
- which columns are in which tables
- column specifications
- view names and definitions
- index names and definitions

Interestingly, although the existence of a System Catalog is one of the requirements of the relational model (see chapter 13), ANSI SQL does not attempt to specify a standard System Catalog! So you will find that the number and names of the tables and columns in the catalog are not standard, and will be different over different SQL implementations. Usually, tables begin with the letters 'SYS'. dBASE IV SQL, for example, has ten tables, called:

```
SYSAUTH    (user privileges on tables and views)
SYSCOLAU   (user privileges on columns)
SYSCOLS    (describes all columns in the database)
SYSIDXS    (describes every index)
SYSKEYS    (describes every column in every index)
SYSSYNS    (synonym definitions)
SYSTABLS   (table descriptions)
SYSTIMES   (multi-user system details)
SYSVDEPS   (describes relationship between tables and views)
SYSVIEWS   (contains view definitions)
```

dBASE also has a 'special' catalog table called SYSDBS, containing a list of all database names. This table is held only in dBASE's SQL Home Directory, and is the one accessed by the SHOW DATABASES command.

Oracle has over 40 tables in the System Catalog!

In every implementation you can view the contents of these tables by using a standard SELECT command (as you would do on normal data tables). For example, dBASE's:

```
SELECT * FROM syscols
         WHERE tbname = 'salesmen';
```

will show you all the column names in the 'salesmen' table.

SQL maintains and updates the system catalog automatically, entering and deleting entries as users create and delete databases, tables and columns. You cannot make entries or change data in the system catalog yourself directly (e.g. by attempting to use a command like INSERT).

4.4 Tables

Before we discuss the CREATE TABLE command in detail, we should point out some of the 'naming conventions' that apply to both table and column names.

4.4.1 Restrictions on table names

Since tables are stored as distinct files under your computer's operating system, they are often subject to the file-naming conventions which the particular computer environment enforces. For example, dBASE IV SQL enforces the PC-DOS file-naming conventions of:

- no more than 8 characters long
- no 'strange' characters (e.g. ', ?, ^)
- no spaces

However, Oracle running on a PC-DOS system holds data in a different way, and imposes no such length restriction on table names.

In addition, you should never use any SQL 'reserved words' – i.e. any word which normally appears as part of an SQL command – as a file name. You may find that your SQL implementation *permits* you to create tables with such names, but if you do, there is always the chance of a subsequent SQL statement being misinterpreted!

4.4.2 Restrictions on column names

As with table names, your particular SQL implementation may impose restrictions on permitted column names. dBASE IV SQL, for example, limits you to 10-character column names (to preserve compatibility with dBASE IV non-SQL files). Consult your system documentation for its particular quirks!

Again, do not use SQL reserved words as column names. It can be very tempting, and apparently innocuous, to define a column with the name 'Date' – perhaps to hold the date on which an employee joined the company. dBASE IV SQL would allow you to do this, but then shower you with (confusing) error messages when you tried to access that column with a SELECT command.

As a general rule, you should use short, but descriptive, names for both tables and columns, since you will find yourself typing them in frequently. If you are worried about the 'unintelligibility' of column names, remember that most SQL implementations include form-building utility programs which will let you create user-friendly reports and input screens for non-technical users.

4.4.3 Restrictions on numbers of columns

This is another implementation-dependent variable. It ranges from 255 (dBASE IV SQL) through to 'unlimited' for Oracle and Informix. However, even 255 columns is likely to be plenty for most applications; indeed, there is a strong argument for saying that in many cases if you think you need more than 255 columns in one table, you have probably got an inefficient database design anyway.

4.4.4 Data types

When you create a table, you have to define for each column the type of data that it will be allowed to hold. This comes down to a basic distinction between **character** data (for example a salesman's name and address), **numeric** data (the salesman's salary), and **date** information (the date he joined the company).

In fact, ANSI standard SQL does not support a 'date' type; however, all SQL implementations offer such a type because of its extreme usefulness! You will find that the various SQL implementations offer some or all of the ANSI data types, as well as some additional ones (like date, time and logical).

Here is a list of the ANSI standard data types.

CHARACTER (length)
NUMERIC (precision, scale)
DECIMAL (precision, scale)
INTEGER

SMALLINT
FLOAT (precision)
REAL
DOUBLE PRECISION

CHARACTER, NUMERIC and INTEGER can be abbreviated to CHAR, NUM and INT (the only occasion when SQL allows abbreviation of commands!).

Another common data type is VARCHAR(length), for Variable Length fields, coming from the DB2 'standard'. Lots of SQL implementations allow this type as a synonym for CHAR.

Character fields

The character column type CHAR(length) stores alphabetic characters.

This does not mean that you cannot enter numbers into a CHAR field; merely that if you do so, those numbers will not be available for calculations. So an 'address' column defined as CHAR(25) could have the value '99, The High Rd.' entered into it.

In many implementations, character data is stored in variable length fields. This means that if you enter only 5 characters in a column defined with a length of 25, then only 5 characters (plus some field overhead) are stored on the disk. Thus, the 'length' parameter is really used to mean 'no more than' this number of letters. However, this does *not* mean that you should lazily define all your character fields as CHAR(1000)! Reasonable values, indicating that some thought has been given to the database design, should always be given.

Numeric fields

As you saw in the list above, there are lots of ways of specifying number data. In fact, the vast majority of numeric data can be represented by the NUMERIC data type.

The format of NUMERIC is:

NUMERIC (total length, decimal places)

The count of total length includes the decimal point. Thus, a column 'salary' defined as 'NUMERIC(8,2)' will allow a salary of 12345.78 (total length 8), but not 12345678.99 (as you might wrongly assume from the definition).

INTEGER and SMALLINT are useful for holding whole numbers which are never going to generate decimal places.

In most cases, the difference between the various ways of holding numeric data is the *maximum size* of the number that can be held, and hence the amount of storage consumed on the disk for each entry. For example, in dBASE IV SQL INTEGER values may be up to 11 digits long (including sign), whereas SMALLINT can hold only 6 digits.

Range

```
INTEGER        -9,999,999,999 to 99,999,999,999
SMALLINT       -99,999 to 999,999
```

Maximum allowable column widths vary between SQL implementations. Check the documentation for any particular system to find out its limitations.

Date fields

Dates are displayed in various implementation-dependent formats. Thus the date of 'December 25th 1990' could appear in any of the following ways:

```
25/12/90          dBASE IV SQL (British)
12/25/90          dBASE IV SQL (American)
25-DEC-90         Oracle
901225            DB2
12-25-1990        Informix
```

In addition, most SQLs provide a 'formatting' option (non-ANSI) to allow dates to be displayed in various different formats.

Internally, all SQLs hold dates as a number, so that you can perform comparisons between them.

4.4.5 Creating a table – CREATE TABLE

Once you have entered SQL and, if necessary, STARTed a database, you can create a table. CREAT(E)ing a table involves giving a name to the table and defining the column names and data types belonging in that table. The format of the standard CREATE TABLE command is:

```
CREATE TABLE tbname (column list [NOT NULL])
      [UNIQUE column list];
```

Some implementations offer other options on CREATE TABLE – for example, Oracle's ability to define the area on disk that this table will occupy (SPACE), the cluster it belongs to (CLUSTER), and even to create a new base table as the result of a SELECT query (AS query). DB2 also allows you to name the *creator* of the table as part of the command (CREATOR), and define DEFAULTs for a column.

Other implementations do not offer the full ANSI standard options – dBASE IV SQL does not implement NULL columns at all. And in most implementations (e.g. DB2, SQL/DS, Oracle, dBASE IV SQL, Informix) the concept of UNIQUEness (see below for full discussion) is carried out in the CREATE INDEX command rather than CREATE TABLE.

Here is the CREATE TABLE command to create the 'salesmen' table that we finally arrived at after our discussion of database design in chapter 3.

```
CREATE TABLE salesmen
    (empno      CHAR(5) NOT NULL,
    surname     CHAR(20),
    firstname   CHAR(15),
    region      CHAR(5),
    datejoined  DATE
    q1target    NUMBER(8,2) NOT NULL,
    q2target    NUMBER(8,2) NOT NULL,
    q3target    NUMBER(8,2) NOT NULL,
    q4target    NUMBER(8,2) NOT NULL
    UNIQUE empno);
```

Notice that we spread the statement over several lines to improve readability. SQL would have been just as happy with the whole lot on one long line.

4.4.5.1 NOT NULL columns
The concept of NULL is discussed in detail in chapter 13 (The Relational Model). A NULL value differs from a blank or zero entry in a column in that it is a 'deliberate' entry showing that the information for this field is unknown.

NULLs are often shown in SQL tables by a question mark '?' or the word 'null', although there is no standard agreed for representing them. Oracle allows you to define whatever character(s) you like for representation of nulls.

Defining a column as NOT NULL means that SQL will not allow NULL values to be entered. In other words, every entry in a NOT NULL column must have a value – which may of course be blanks or zero.

The aim of this is to try to force users to enter data into 'essential' columns. In the salesmen table above, the user will have to at least *consider* entering data for the salesman's name and his four target figures.

The power of NOT NULL is considerably enhanced when used in conjunction with the UNIQUE option (see below).

4.4.5.2 UNIQUE columns
UNIQUE is used to prevent duplicate entries in 'essential' columns. For example, in the 'salesmen' table each employee number should be unique – two employees *never* have the same employee number.

The ANSI standard allows you to specify any column or combination of columns as UNIQUE. Every such column must also be specified as NOT NULL.

4.4.5.3 UNIQUEness in different SQLs – INDEX vs TABLE

Specifying a column combination as UNIQUE when the table is created is clearly the best way to ensure that no duplicate rows are ever included. However, as we mentioned above, most SQLs currently implement UNIQUE-ness in an index rather than on the table itself. A brief explanation of the term INDEX is given in chapter 3; indexes are discussed in more detail in chapter 9.

So Oracle, for example, would create the salesmen table as we did above, but without the 'UNIQUE empno' clause. The Oracle user would then have to create an index as:

```
CREATE UNIQUE INDEX salesemp
    ON salesmen (empno);
```

Although this dual operation has the same net effect as specifying 'UNIQUE empno' on the table itself, it is inherently more clumsy and less indicative of the real situation – surely UNIQUEness is a property of the table, not of a subsequent index.

However, the fact remains that, whether or not it is the most desirable way of guaranteeing non-duplicate rows, most of the most reputable SQLs *do* use this method. This is an example of the ANSI standard being very different – albeit 'better' – from most actual implementations. Check the documentation carefully for any particular implementation to see how it implements UNIQUEness. It may be the case that suppliers will eventually enhance their SQL systems to include the ANSI standard UNIQUE.

4.4.6 Changing the structure of a table – ALTER TABLE

The ANSI standard contains no command for changing the structure of a table! However, you will find that there is a de facto standard among SQLs, taken from DB2.

The ALTER TABLE command can be used to *add* a column to a table, and (in some implementations) to *modify* a column specification. It is not used to delete a column. To delete a column you have to create a new table without the offending column specification, and then transfer data from the old table to the new one, probably with the INSERT INTO..SELECT ..command. See chapter 8 for a full discussion.

The format of ALTER TABLE is:

```
ALTER TABLE tbname
    ADD (column spec);
```

To add a column 'Region' to the salesmen table we would say:

```
ALTER TABLE salesmen
        ADD (region CHAR(4));
```

You specify the new column in exactly the same way as you specified columns in CREATE TABLE.

4.4.6.1 Adding NOT NULL columns

If you add a column, SQL automatically fills it with NULL for all existing rows. It is impossible to specify an ADDed column directly as NOT NULL – because SQL obviously cannot fill in correct values by itself!

Oracle will allow you to ADD a NOT NULL column only if there are no rows in the table; other implementations such as DB2 will not permit even this.

There are various techniques for adding NOT NULL columns, involving creating a new table with the desired structure and then transferring over the rows from the old table. This technique is described in detail in chapter 8.

4.4.6.2 Modifying a column specification

Modifying a column specification means renaming the column, changing the column width, or changing the data type. DB2 and its followers have no way to do this other than to create a new table with the desired structure, and use INSERT to transfer rows.

Oracle has the useful MODIFY clause available in the ALTER TABLE command to allow column widths to be increased. To increase the width of the salemen's address to 35 characters, the Oracle user could say:

```
ALTER TABLE salesmen
        MODIFY (address CHAR(35))
```

However, you cannot decrease column widths if there are non-null values in the column.

4.5 Inputting data – INSERT..VALUES

Once the table has been created to your satisfaction, you can start inputting rows of data.

SQL has several commands allowing data rows to be added to a table. The simplest, and the one dealt with here, lets the user himself type in the data items for each column, one row at a time. This is the INSERT command. Other commands such as LOAD DATA, INPUT, and also more complex usage of INSERT (using subqueries), are dealt with in chapter 8.

The format for the basic INSERT command is:

```
INSERT INTO tbname (columnlist) VALUES (value list);
```

4.5.1 *Inserting a whole row*

To insert a row into the salesmen table, we would say:

```
INSERT INTO salesmen VALUES
        ('10001',
         'Smith',
         'John',
         'East',
         '01-123-4567',
         TO_DATE('01-JAN-89'),
         50000,
         50000,
         75000,
         100000);
```

Data items are 'fed into' consecutive columns, so you have to make sure that you enter the column contents in the correct order.

If a column is defined as NOT NULL, you *must* enter a value for it; otherwise SQL will give you an error message on the lines of Oracle's 'mandatory (NOT NULL) column is missing or NULL during insert'.

4.5.2 *Inserting values into specific columns*

If you do not want to put data in *all* the columns of a new row, you can specify exactly which columns are to be updated. Again, the data items are assigned consecutively to the columns that you specify.

```
        INSERT INTO salesmen
  (empno,q1target,q2target,q3target,q4target)
        VALUES
        ('12345',
        50000,
        50000,
        75000,
        100000);
```

Most SQL implementations automatically assign a NULL value to columns not specified in the list.

4.5.3 *Problems with INSERT*

In practice, this method of entering data is clumsy and long-winded, and not recommended for most users. This is definitely one of the areas where the form-design utilities available with most SQLs come into their own. Alternatively, you could embed the INSERT statement within a programming language, using the language to prompt intelligibly for inputs.

INSERT can also be used with a SELECT subquery to transfer rows from one table to another. This is discussed fully in chapter 8.

4.6 Deleting a table – DROP TABLE

This is another feature not mentioned in the ANSI standard, but which exists in most implementations anyway.

The command to delete a table is simply:

```
DROP TABLE tbname;
```

So we could delete our 'salesmen' table by saying:

```
DROP TABLE salesmen;
```

All references to this table (and any associated views and indexes) are automatically removed from the system catalogs.

Summary

In this chapter we looked at setting up an SQL system. You learned how start and finish an SQL session, manipulate databases, create a table, type in rows of data (using the simplest of the possible SQL commands available), and delete a table.

In the next chapter we will consider how to query data with the SELECT command.

5 *Querying the database*

Overview

This chapter deals with retrieving data once it has been entered into a table or tables.

You will learn how to perform simple queries on a single table, extracting information both by column and by row. We will look at sequencing results in a particular order, and summarising results. We will also start to look at extracting data from more than one table simultaneously.

Chapter 6 deals in more detail with using multiple tables, and more complex uses of SELECT, including the GROUP BY, HAVING and UNION clauses.

Major commands covered in this chapter

SELECT..
FROM
WHERE
ORDER BY

5.1 Introduction

Retrieving data is one of the key areas in any database system. What good is a database language which cannot 'get back' the data in a comprehensive fashion to suit all needs? You will see here that SQL's query facilities are extremely powerful. The remarkable thing (especially so for those people coming to SQL from using a more limited data retrieval language such as dBASE III) is that complex queries involving multiple tables, summaries and sorting, can all be carried out by one 'interactive' command. In other words, there should be little need for any SQL user to have to resort to programming in order to extract the data that he requires. (Remember, though, that we are talking here about getting the required results into a result table; formatting them for reports may well involve some programming, or at least the use of a 4GL design utility.)

5.2 The SELECT command – an introductory look

SQL's query command is called SELECT. The syntax of SELECT, and the various options it offers, are one of the few areas where most implementations agree with each other and even with the ANSI standard! This is just as well, since SELECT is so vital to SQL's success as a database language. However, some SQLs offer 'extra' SELECT options over the standard – for example dBASE IV SQL's SAVE TO TEMP or Informix's INTO TEMP clause (both of which convert the result table into a 'real' data table).

SELECT is used to 'extract' rows and columns from 'real' tables into a temporary 'result' table. The result table may just display on the screen; it may be 'fed into' a predefined report; or it may itself be converted to a 'real' table for further querying.

The syntax of the SELECT command is:

```
SELECT (DISTINCT | ALL)
[* | column list]
FROM  tablename(s) (alias ..)
WHERE condition
GROUP BY column list
HAVING condition
ORDER BY column list (ASC|DESC)
UNION query
```

Although this looks rather alarming at first sight, the use of all the component clauses is really very easy to grasp. The first thing to realise is that you do not have to use all the clauses all the time! The only *essential* elements of a SELECT statement are the clauses telling SQL which columns to extract from which tables(s); in other words, just SELECT..FROM.. A typical SELECT statement to show the surnames of all salesmen would simply say:

```
SELECT surname FROM salesmen;
```

5.2.1 Brief explanation of the function of each clause

Here is a brief explanation of the functions of each clause in the SELECT statement. This should give you a feel for what it is possible to achieve using SELECT. At the end of the explanation for each clause is an example of its use, building up gradually to a full SELECT statement.

In the next section we will consider each part of the SELECT statement in more detail.

1. SELECT (DISTINCT I ALL) [* I column list]
This part of the command tells SQL which columns to put in the result table
(* I column list), and whether or not to include rows containing repeated
identical column values (DISTINCT I ALL).

The column list for the result table is a simple list of columns separated
by commas. Columns can be specified in any order. You can also include
'calculated' columns, columns to which a 'function' (usually non-standard
SQL) has been applied, and aggregate functions (SUM, MIN, MAX etc).

The asterisk * can be used as 'shorthand' to mean *all* columns in the
order in which they appear in the base table.

Example: SELECT empno,surname,q1target

(Note that by itself this is not a valid SQL statement since it does not
include the FROM clause.)

2. FROM tablename(s) (alias ..)
This clause specifies the tables from which data will be retrieved. If data is
needed from more than one table, you separate table names with a comma.

Example: SELECT empno,surname,q1target,region
              FROM salesmen;

to see the employee number, surname, region and Quarter 1 target for all
rows in the 'salesmen' table. The result table would look like this (assuming
that there are five salesmen in the company!):

Empno	Surname	Q1target	Region
10001	Smith	50000	East
40004	Jones	25000	West
20002	Brown	40000	East
30003	Adams	50000	South
50005	James	60000	East

When you use multiple tables, you may find it useful to set up aliases for
table names – usually *shorter* names by which you can refer to your tables
for the duration of the query. We deal with multiple tables and aliases in
chapter 6.

3. WHERE condition
A WHERE condition is used to restrict the rows which appear in the result
table. Only rows for which the condition evaluates as TRUE will be passed
to the result table.

Conditions can include arithmetic operators (=, <>, <, > etc), logical operators (AND, OR, NOT), and other 'special' operators (IN, LIKE, BETWEEN etc).

WHERE conditions may also include 'nested' subqueries (i.e. another SELECT statement). This is dealt with fully in section 6.6.

Example: SELECT empno,surname,q1target,region
                     FROM salesmen
                     WHERE region = 'East';

to restrict the result table to only the salesmen in East Region:

```
Empno Surname      Q1target   Region
------------------------------------
10001 Smith          50000     East
20002 Brown          40000     East
50005 James          60000     East
```

4. ORDER BY column list (ASC|DESC)

ORDER BY is used to sequence the rows of the result table in the 'order' that you require. You can order a table based on any column or combination of columns, in ascending or descending order. Columns are sorted in ASCending order by default.

Example: SELECT empno, surname, q1target FROM salesmen
                     WHERE region = 'East'
                     ORDER BY q1target DESC;

to see all salesmen in West Region, showing the one with the highest Quarter 1 target first.

Result table:

```
Empno Surname      Q1target   Region
------------------------------------
50005 James          60000     East
10001 Smith          50000     East
20002 Brown          40000     East
```

5. GROUP BY column list

GROUP BY is used to create summaries of data based on row groupings.

In the result table, each group is reduced to a single row.

GROUP BY is often used with one or more of the **aggregate functions** (COUNT, SUM, AVG, MAX, MIN) in the 'SELECT column list' clause. This is because a common reason for grouping rows is to find out totals

(SUM), maximums and minimums in the group (MAX, MIN), the precise number of rows in each group (COUNT), etc.

There are strict rules to describe which columns can be included in the 'SELECT column list' when a GROUP BY is also in effect. These will be discussed in detail in section 6.2.

Here is a SELECT to show the total Quarter 1 target for each sales region, with the three resulting rows shown alphabetically by region.

Example:

```
SELECT region, SUM(q1target) FROM salesmen
      GROUP BY region
      ORDER BY region;
```

Result table:

Region	SUM(q1target)
East	150000
South	50000
West	25000

6. HAVING condition

HAVING is a 'WHERE-clause for groups' (Date, 1988). Use it in conjunction with the GROUP BY clause to restrict the groups which appear in the result table.

Usually a HAVING clause performs a condition check on one or more of the column values included in the SELECT column list.

Example:

```
SELECT region, SUM(q1target) FROM salesmen
      GROUP BY region
      HAVING SUM(q1target) > 25000
      ORDER BY region;
```

to see the region and total Quarter 1 target for only those sales regions for which the target is greater than 25000.

Result table:

Region	SUM(q1target)
East	150000
South	50000

7. UNION query

UNION allows you to combine the resulting rows from two or more totally separate queries into the same result table.

UNION is always followed by another SELECT statement.

Using UNION can give similar results to using an OR condition in a WHERE clause. However, the ANSI standard uses opposite conventions for the defaults for DISTINCT and ALL in SELECT and UNION clauses, which can make a considerable difference to the result tables produced by the two different methods. SELECT assumes a default of ALL; UNION assumes a default of DISTINCT. In other words, all duplicate rows are eliminated in a UNION statement unless you specifically demand ALL rows, whereas in a WHERE..OR.. condition they would automatically be retained.

Example:

```
SELECT empno,surname,q1target FROM salesmen;
     WHERE region = 'West';
     UNION
          SELECT empno,surname,q1target FROM salesmen
          WHERE q1target > 50000
     ORDER BY empno;
```

to show all salesmen in West Region, *and* all salesmen for whom the Quarter 1 target is greater than 50000, with the result table sorted in employee number order.

Empno	Surname	Q1target	Region
40004	Jones	25000	West
50005	James	60000	East

5.2.2 Essential points about SELECT

Here is a summary of the three most important points to note regarding the SELECT syntax:

1. Only the first two clauses – i.e. the SELECT..FROM.. – are essential. Everything else is optional.
2. The clauses must *always* be used in the order given above. You cannot, for example, put ORDER BY immediately after SELECT, or immediately before GROUP BY. However, you can of course leave out the WHERE, GROUP BY and HAVING clauses altogether, and have ORDER BY immediately following FROM.
3. HAVING should only be used if there is also a GROUP BY clause. (The ANSI standard does actually allow HAVING to be used without GROUP BY, but this then makes it equivalent to WHERE. Many SQL implementations do not support this usage.)

5.3 Using SELECT

Now that you have an idea of the scope of SELECT, let us look in more detail at what each element of the statement can be used to achieve.

We will not cover all the complexities of all the clauses in this one chapter. We will leave discussion of multiple tables until chapter 6, and we will also talk there about GROUP BY, HAVING, and UNION.

So this chapter will cover the basic SELECT statement, to get you to the point where you can form a query to retrieve the required columns and rows, and sequence them in the order that you need.

The 'simple' SELECT statement – SELECT..FROM..

Let us look first at what can be done with the only essential parts of a SELECT statement – the SELECT..FROM.. . Here are some examples of valid SELECTs. All of these copy *all* the rows in the base table to the result table.

```
SELECT *  FROM salesmen;
```

(shows all columns).

```
SELECT empno,q1target,surname FROM salesmen;
```

(shows only employee number, Quarter 1 target, and salesman's surname).

```
SELECT surname,q1target,q1target*1.1 FROM salesmen;
```

(shows salesman's surname, Quarter 1 target, and the calculated value of target + 10%).

```
SELECT surname,q1target+q2target+q3target+q4target
    FROM salesmen;
```

(shows salesman's surname, and the total target for the entire year).

5.3.1 Manipulating NUMBERs

You can see from the above examples that you can use standard arithmetic operators (+ − * /) to perform 'temporary' calculations on base table numeric data. The answers appear in the result table, but of course are not saved permanently in the base table. Such calculated columns usually appear in the result table with a column heading the same as the 'calculation expression' in the SELECT column list. This can look extremely unwieldy – as it would for the 'total target' example above – but remember that you could easily feed this result into a predefined report form which would format the result table in a more 'user friendly' fashion.

5.3.2 *Manipulating characters and dates (functions)*

All SQL implementations also provide ways of changing the amount of
character and date type data between the base and the result tables – for
example, to copy over only the last three characters of employee numbers,
or only the year from a date. These manipulative commands are normally
referred to as **functions**. However, ANSI SQL includes *no* such functions in
the standard.

Similarly, most SQLs have formatting commands to change the display
format of data – for example, to show dates in British format DD/MM/YY
rather than most implementations' standard American MM/DD/YY, or to
convert all data to upper case display. ANSI SQL does not include any of
these either.

You will therefore find that, although similar facilities occur over all
implementations and although they can be essential in producing the desired
output, there is no agreement over exactly what functions should be provided,
nor over what their syntax should be.

For that reason, this book makes very little mention of functions and
formatting commands. You should, however, remember that they exist, and
check out the full list available in the documentation of any particular SQL
system.

5.3.3 *Restrictions on column lists*

The ANSI standard does not allow you to use both the asterisk (all
columns) *and* a column specification. So a command like:

```
SELECT *, qltarget*1.1 FROM salesmen;        ** ILLEGAL **
```

is illegal. However, many SQLs, including DB2, *do* allow such a construction.

5.3.4 *Aggregate functions*

ANSI SQL provides five functions which summarise values from the whole
table. These are:

COUNT(*)	(number of rows)
SUM (column list)	(total value)
MAX "	(maximum value)
MIN "	(minimum value)
AVG "	(average value)

All these can be used with or without the DISTINCT option (see 5.3.5). These can be included in the SELECT column list. For example, you could say

```
SELECT MAX(q1target),MIN(q1target),AVG(q1target)
     FROM salesmen;
```

to show the highest, lowest and average target figures respectively.

Result table:

MAX(q1target)	MIN(q1target)	AVG(q1target)
60000	25000	45000

To see the number of salesmen in the table and the total expected quarter 1 targets you could say:

```
SELECT COUNT(*), SUM(q1target) FROM salesmen;
```

Result table:

COUNT(*)	SUM(q1target)
5	225000

The aggregate functions are especially useful when used in the GROUP BY clause, and in WHERE subqueries (see chapter 6).

5.3.5 Using DISTINCT

The DISTINCT option allows you to specify that you want to see only the *first* occurrence of the column or combination of columns specified in the 'column list'. No repeated values are included. For example, if a newcomer to the company wanted to see how many different sales region codes were in use, he could say:

```
SELECT DISTINCT region FROM salesmen;
```

and get a result table showing four rows containing respectively 'North', 'South', 'West', and 'East'.

Using ALL instead of DISTINCT in an otherwise identical query would give a fairly meaningless result showing the region from all rows in the base table.

In fact, SQL assumes a default of ALL. So you will not usually see the word ALL included in SELECT statements, although there is no harm in putting it in if you want to be sure that you and other users understand exactly what is intended by a particular statement.

DISTINCT is often used with the aggregate functions COUNT(*), SUM, MIN, MAX and AVG, since it provides an easy way to filter out duplicates from summaries. For example:

```
SELECT SUM(DISTINCT q1target) FROM salesmen;
```

to total all target figures with different values.

We will discuss other uses of DISTINCT in the next chapter.

5.3.6 Aliases and multiple tables

At this stage in a SELECT statement you can tell SQL to extract data from several tables instead of just one and, to save yourself extra typing, you can also specify an alias for a table (usually a 'short' name by which you can refer to the table for the duration of this query). We will deal with multiple table queries in chapter 6.

5.4 WHERE conditions

5.4.1 What is a WHERE condition?

A WHERE clause sets a *condition* which defines the rows to be passed to the result table.

There are very few situations where you want to see *all* rows in a table, so in practice most SELECT statements have a WHERE clause attached to them.

WHERE conditions compare a column value against either a constant, another column value, or an expression. For example:

```
SELECT surname FROM salesmen
       WHERE q1target = 100000;
```
Constant

```
SELECT surname FROM salesmen
       WHERE q1target > q4target
```
Column value

```
SELECT surname FROM salesmen
       WHERE q1target < (q4target/1.75)
```
Expression

The result of a condition will be either TRUE, FALSE or NULL for each row in the base table. For example, if q1target contains the value 50000, then the condition

```
.. q1target = 50000
```

is TRUE, whereas the condition

```
.. qltarget = 100000
```

is FALSE.

If q1target contained a NULL value, then the result of the condition

```
.. qltarget = 50000
```

is NULL.

As a general rule, only rows for which a condition evaluates as TRUE are passed to the result table. You can also include a check for NULL or NOT NULL values in a condition (see below).

WHEREs can become quite complex. As we mentioned above there are lots of operators which can apply to a WHERE condition. You can also set up subqueries to compare a result with another set of data.

We will discuss the various WHERE operators in some detail in this chapter. The topic of subqueries will be touched on here, but dealt with in more detail in chapter 6, since in most cases subqueries involve accessing data from more than one table.

5.4.2 The WHERE operators

Here is a summary of the comparison operators and operations available in WHERE clauses. We will give examples of each one in the following sections.

- simple comparisons (=, <, > etc)
- BETWEEN value1 AND value2
- IN (list)
- LIKE mask
- IS NULL
- NOT (expression)
- 'linked' conditions (AND, OR)
- subquery operators: EXISTS, ANY, ALL IN

Arithmetic comparisons
Probably the majority of your SQL queries will use simple 'arithmetic' operators in comparisons. For example, to see all salesmen for whom the Quarter 1 target is £100000, you say:

```
SELECT surname FROM salesmen
     WHERE qltarget = 100000;
```

You could actually reverse the order of the WHERE comparison to read

```
SELECT surname FROM salesmen
        WHERE 100000 = q1target;
```

and get precisely the same result, although the first order seems more 'Englishlike' and natural.

The complete list of arithmetic operators is:

=	is equal to
>	is greater than
<	is less than
>=	is greater than or equal to
<=	is less than or equal to
<>	is not equal to

Some SQL implementations also allow you to use '!=' and/or '^=' to mean 'is not equal to'.

Of course, 'arithmetic' operators are not restricted to working only on NUMBER data. They can be used for CHARACTER data, as well as most of the non-ANSI data types.

Comparing different data types
Note that you cannot compare data of different data types (with the exception of the various number-based data types) against each other. So all the following comparisons would produce an error message

```
SELECT surname FROM salesmen
        WHERE surname = 100000          (character vs number)

  ..    WHERE surname = Smith           (no quotes round 'Smith')

  ..    WHERE q1target > datejoined     (number vs date)
```

Fortunately, most such data-type comparisons are obviously nonsensical – no-one would deliberately compare 'q1target' with 'datejoined'!

Problems usually arise either when you are not sure of a column's data type and the name gives no clue to the type of information that it may contain (e.g. a column with the name 'c1'), or when you specify a constant incorrectly (e.g. forgetting to put quotation marks around a character string). Avoid the first type of problem by giving columns sensible descriptive names – 'address' rather than 'c1'. You can of course check the data type of a column in the System Catalog (see chapter 4).

Comparing number data
Numbers are 'sequenced' in the 'natural' order. Thus **1** is smaller than **10**; **10** is greater than **0**, and **0** is greater than **-1**.

You can validly compare number-based data of different data types – for example, SMALLINT data against INTEGER, or DECIMAL with NUMERIC.

Comparing character strings
Character strings are compared character by character on a left to right basis. In other words, when sorting character data, the system first checks the first letter in the column, and sorts the rows on that basis. If more than one row has identical first letters in the specified column, then the system proceeds to sort this group by the second character – and so it continues until all rows are in the correct sequence.

With CHARACTER data, the meaning of 'less than', 'greater than' etc becomes less obvious. The = clearly still means 'is the same as', as in:

```
SELECT surname, qltarget FROM salesmen
       WHERE surname = 'Smith';
```
(to see details for John Smith only)

and the <> still means 'is not the same as', as in

```
SELECT surname, qltarget FROM salesmen
       WHERE surname <> 'Smith';
```
(to see details for all salesmen *except* John Smith).

However, the 'sequencing' of alphanumeric characters – i.e. which are the 'smallest' and which the 'largest' – varies according to the computer environment on which a particular implementation is running. Most computer systems use either the **ASCII** (American Standard Code for Information Interchange) or the **EBDCIC** (Extended Binary Coded Data Interchange Code) character set. The same set of characters is available in both sets but sequenced in a different order. As a rule of thumb, MS-DOS or PC-DOS systems will use the ASCII character set; IBM mainframe-based systems will probably use EBCDIC. The most obvious difference is that EBCDIC considers lower case characters to be 'smaller' than upper case ones, whereas ASCII sorts them the other way round. See the tables below.

Alphanumeric comparison order – ASCII
Value in column

Smallest	blank
	0 – 9
	A – Z (upper case alphabetic characters)
Largest	a – z (lower case alphabetic characters)

Thus lower case **a** is 'greater than' upper case **A**.

Alphanumeric comparison order – EBCDIC
Value in column

Smallest	blank
↓	a – z
	A – Z
Largest	0 – 9

Thus lower case **a** is 'smaller than' upper case **A**.

There is no 'rule' that either ASCII or EBCDIC should be used, and you may well find that yet another character set, and hence yet another sorting sequence, may be used on your particular computer.

This means, of course, that you could run an identical query on identical data on three different computers, and end up with three different results!

Using functions to ensure correct sorting of character data
The most common area where this causes problems is in the sequencing or retrieving of alphabetic data. In most cases, users consider that upper case and lower case letters are functionally equivalent. In other words, **a** is the same as **A**. A query like:

```
SELECT surname FROM salesmen
     WHERE surname > 'Smith'
```

should show you 'Thomas', 'Zebedee' and 'williams', but *not* 'smith' and 'adams'.

The non-standard SQL commands available in all SQL implementations usually provide a way of telling SQL to treat upper and lower case as the same. Often this involves use of a function which the user has to specify in the query. For example, both dBASE IV SQL and Oracle would allow you to say

```
SELECT surname FROM salesmen
     WHERE upper(surname) > 'SMITH';
```

which, for the duration of this query only, 'converts' all surnames in the table to upper case.

You should check the documentation of your particular SQL implementation to see how it recommends that you cope with this type of problem.

NULLs in comparisons
Whether a NULL value is considered to be the 'lowest' or the 'highest' value in comparisons depends on the particular SQL implementation. dBASE

IV doesn't implement NULLs at all anyway, so it does not have to cope with the problem. Oracle puts NULL values before blanks.

Comparing dates
In date comparisons, as you would expect, earlier dates appear before later dates. Thus **01/01/80** is 'smaller than' **01/01/90**.

5.4.3 BETWEEN..AND..

BETWEEN allows you to easily specify a *range* in a condition. For example, to retrieve the surnames of all salesmen for whom the target falls between 50000 and 150000, you could say

```
SELECT surname FROM salesmen
    WHERE qltarget BETWEEN 50000 AND 150000
```

Notice that this is equivalent to a WHERE clause using arithmetic operators linked with an AND condition (see 5.4.8 for further discussion of AND)

```
SELECT surname FROM salesmen
    WHERE qltarget >= 50000 AND qltarget <= 150000;
```

BETWEEN simply provides a much more self-explanatory and shorter method of achieving the same result.
 BETWEEN can be used with all data types.

5.4.4 LIKE mask

LIKE allows you to select character strings which, although not identical, still have some element in common. For example, you may want to retrieve the surnames of all salesmen who live in postal district 'W1' – which is stored not in a separate column but as part of the address field. Or you may want to find every employee number ending in '100'.
 To achieve this, you define a **mask** (sometimes called a template) around which the data can fit. A mask uses **wild cards** (similar in operation to those used in filenames by the MS-DOS operating system). This lets you specify which elements of a character string are essential for a successful data match.
 The characters used to mean 'wild card' may vary between SQL implementations. Oracle uses % to mean 'zero, one or more characters', and _ to mean 'one single character'. Informix uses * and ?. You can combine these two wild cards in any order to specify quite complex masks.
 Note that % and _ only have the meaning of 'wild card' when found with the LIKE operator. A query using, for example, the = operator will look for the precise characters '%' and '_' as part of the *data*. For example,

```
SELECT surname FROM salesmen
      WHERE empno = '%100';
```

will look for – and probably not find – an employee number of '%100'.

Examples of LIKE

```
SELECT surname FROM salesmen
      WHERE empno LIKE '%100';
```

(to show all salesmen whose employee number ends in '100').

```
SELECT surname FROM salesmen
      WHERE address LIKE '%W1%';
```

(to show all salesmen whose address contains the character string 'W1').

```
SELECT surname FROM salesmen
      WHERE empno LIKE '1_3_5';
```

(to show all salesmen whose employee number contains the numbers 1, 3, and 5 in the first, third and fifth positions, and anything at all in the second and fourth positions).

```
SELECT surname FROM salesmen
      WHERE empno LIKE '1_3%';
```

(to show all salesmen whose employee number contains '1' in the first position, '3' in the third, and anything at all in the second position, and in positions four and five).

LIKE cannot be used with NUMBER data.

5.4.5 IN (list)

IN, like BETWEEN, is a way of simplifying a condition which otherwise would contain multiple linked ANDs and ORs. IN lets you specify a list of values against which the column value in the WHERE clause is to be compared. For example, to see all employees in 'East' and 'West' sales regions, you could say:

```
SELECT surname FROM employee
      WHERE region IN ('East','West');
```

To see all salesmen whose target is either 50000, 75000 or 200000, you would say

```
SELECT surname FROM salesmen
      WHERE q1target IN (50000, 75000, 200000);
```

An alternative, but more clumsy, way of getting the same result would be the query:

```
SELECT surname FROM salesmen
      WHERE q1target = 50000 OR
      q1target = 75000 OR
      q1target = 200000;
```

IN can be used with all data types.

5.4.6 IS NULL

IS NULL is used to check whether a column contains NULL values. For example, you could find out if any addresses are NULL with the query:

```
SELECT surname FROM salesmen
      WHERE address IS NULL;
```

5.4.7 NOT (expression)

All the WHERE operators apart from the 'arithmetic' operators can be 'negated' by preceding them with NOT. For example

```
SELECT surname FROM salesmen
      WHERE surname NOT LIKE 'S%';
```

(to show all salesmen whose surname *does not* begin with S).

```
SELECT surname FROM salesmen
      WHERE region NOT IN ('East', 'West');
```

(to show everyone in regions other than East or West).

```
SELECT surname FROM salesmen
      WHERE address IS NOT NULL;
```

(to show everyone who has a 'positive' entry in the address column).

Although you cannot use NOT directly in front of arithmetic operators (for example, a construction such as

```
SELECT surname FROM salesmen
      WHERE q1target NOT > 100000           ** ILLEGAL **
```

is WRONG)

you *can* use NOT to negate entire expressions containing arithmetic or other operators. For example:

```
SELECT surname FROM salesmen
    WHERE NOT (q1target = 50000 OR surname = 'Smith');
```

(to show everyone who is not called 'Smith', who has a target different from 50000).

```
SELECT surname FROM salesmen
    WHERE NOT (q1target > 50000);
```

5.4.8 AND and OR

Any valid conditions created using the operators we have already discussed can be 'linked together' by AND and OR.

AND and OR have slightly different interpretations from what might be regarded as their normal 'English' usage. If you have not come across this type of condition before, you may find yourself confused as to their effect.

Let us take a simple two-part condition to illustrate the difference between these two operators. Here is a query repeated twice, once with AND and once with OR.

AND
```
SELECT *  FROM salesmen
    WHERE q1target = 50000
    AND region = 'East';
```

Result table:

Empno	Surname	Q1target	Region
10001	Smith	50000	East

(shows all salesmen in East Region who have a target of 50000).

A row will be passed to the result table only if *all* conditions evaluate as TRUE.

OR
```
SELECT * FROM salesmen
    WHERE q1target = 50000
    OR region = 'East';
```

Result table:

```
Empno Surname     Qltarget    Region
-------------------------------------
10001 Smith        50000       East
20002 Brown        40000       East
30003 Adams        50000       South
```

(shows all salesmen in East Region regardless of target, and also salesmen in any region with a target of 50000).

A row will be passed to the result table if *any* of the conditions evaluate as TRUE.

Conditions linked with AND are more restricting (i.e. allow fewer rows through to the result table) than those linked with OR.

Here are some more examples of linked conditions. Note that these examples use all ANDs or all ORs. The next section looks at the effect of mixing ANDs and ORs.

ORs

```
SELECT surname FROM salesmen
      WHERE qltarget = 50000
      OR region = 'West'
      OR surname LIKE 'S%';
```

(shows all salesmen in West Region regardless of target, *and also* salesmen in any region with a target of 50000, *and also* all salesmen whose surname begins with 'S').

ANDs

```
SELECT surname FROM salesmen
      WHERE qltarget = 50000
      AND region = 'West'
      AND surname LIKE 'S%';
```

(shows salesmen in West Region whose surname begins with 'S', and who have a target of 50000).

Using several ANDs and ORs
You can link together any number of conditions with any combination of AND and OR. For example:

```
SELECT surname FROM salesmen
      WHERE qltarget = 50000
      OR region = 'West'
      AND surname LIKE 'S%';
```

However, this immediately becomes confusing to interpret, because it is not obvious how the conditions are to be grouped. Will this query produce

1. – all salesmen with a target of 50000 *and also*
   – all salesmen in West Region with a surname beginning with 'S'

or

2. – all salesmen whose surname begins with 'S' *and who*
   – either have a target of 50000 or are in West Region?

They could be very different result tables!

Unfortunately, the various SQL implementations disagree on how to 'parse' statements containing multiple ANDs and ORs. Some SQLs work on a straight 'left-to-right' basis. Others, including Oracle and dBASE IV SQL, evaluate all AND clauses before all OR clauses. The two approaches yield different results. The 'left-to-right' evaluation order produces Answer 2; the AND-has-precedence evaluation order produces Answer 1.

Here are worked examples of the logical steps that SQL takes to evaluate the condition in both cases.

1. Method 1 – LEFT-TO-RIGHT

	Condition	SQL's Action
Step 1	q1target = 50000	Place in result table all rows where target is 50000
Step 2	OR region = 'West'	Also place in result table all rows where region is 'West'
Step 3	AND surname LIKE 'S%'	Check all rows in result table and remove those where the surname does not begin with 'S'

2. Method 2 – AND clauses have precedence

	Condition	SQL's Action
Step 1	region = 'West'	Place in result table all rows where region contains 'West'
Step 2	AND surname LIKE 'S%'	Remove those rows from result table where the surname does not begin with 'S'
Step 3	OR q1target = 50000	Also place in result table all rows where target = 50000

Make sure that you find out which method your particular SQL implementation uses; if necessary, by constructing some test data and trying out various queries yourself.

Even better, use brackets to force any SQL to evaluate the condition in the order you need.

Using brackets in conditions

You can use **brackets** to force SQL to evaluate linked conditions in the order that you require. SQL evaluates bracketed conditions first, and then applies a left-to-right evaluation order on the results. In the above example, to be sure that any SQL implementation will produce Answer 2 rather than Answer 1, you could say

```
SELECT surname FROM salesmen
    WHERE (qltarget = 50000
    OR region = 'West')
    AND surname LIKE 'S%';
```

Using brackets makes the intended result of a condition clearer, even if the brackets are merely used to confirm the 'natural' evaluation order. So, to produce Answer 2 using Oracle, it would be better to include brackets for clarity's sake:

```
SELECT surname FROM salesmen
    WHERE qltarget = 50000
    OR (region = 'West'
    AND surname LIKE 'S%');
```

5.4.9 Simple subqueries

You can get SQL to perform another SELECT statement as part of the WHERE clause, and to compare a column value against the result table of that secondary SELECT. The second SELECT is known as a **subquery**.

Subqueries can act either on the same table as the main SELECT, or on a different table (or tables). At this point we will only deal with subqueries on the same table. See chapter 6 for a full discussion of multiple table operations.

There are two kinds of subqueries: those which return a single value, and those which return multiple values. Those returning a single value need no special syntax in addition to the operators that we have already covered; those returning multiple values make use of the subquery operators IN, EXISTS, ANY and ALL.

In this chapter we will only discuss those simple subqueries which return a single value. See chapter 6 for a more in-depth treatment of subqueries.

You would need a subquery, for example, to find all salesmen who have the same Quarter 1 target as John Smith. Using a subquery effectively lets you use a single SQL statement to make two passes through the salesmen table – first to find John Smith's target, and secondly to compare each row's target figure against John Smith's. The SQL command to achieve this is shown below.

Example:

```
SELECT surname FROM salesmen
      WHERE q1target =
      (SELECT q1target FROM salesmen
      WHERE surname = 'Smith');
```

(to show all salesmen whose target is the same as John Smith's).

The subquery must be enclosed within brackets. Notice that this subquery returns a single value.

How queries containing subqueries are evaluated
When presented with a condition containing a subquery, SQL evaluates the subquery first. It then 'feeds in' the values returned in the subquery's result table into the main condition.

SQL evaluates the query above as:

	Condition	SQL's Action
Step 1	surname = 'Smith'	Place in an 'temporary' result table the q1target value for the row where surname = 'Smith'
Step 2	q1target = SELECT..	Place in the final result table all rows where q1target is the same as the value in the temporary result table.

The subquery can be a complex condition using ANDs, ORs etc. It may itself contain a subquery. If there are several subqueries in a statement, the one nested 'deepest' is evaluated first.

You should indent your SQL statements to make the intended evaluation order clearer. For example

```
SELECT surname FROM salesmen
      WHERE q1target IN
      (SELECT q1target FROM salesmen
      WHERE datejoined >
      (SELECT avg(datejoined) FROM salesmen));
```

to show salesmen whose target is the same as that of any salesman who joined the company after the average joining date!

We will talk more about subqueries in the next chapter.

5.5 ORDER BY column list (DESC)

This clause allows you to sequence the rows in the result table. Rows can be 'ordered' on any single column or combination of columns.

Rows are normally sequenced in ascending order. You can change this by specifying the DESC option with ORDER BY.

The rules for determining which values are the smallest and which the largest, and for treatment of NULL values, are the same as those discussed in section 5.4.2 when we talked about the arithmetic operators.

5.5.1 *Ordering by a single column*

This very simple method of sorting the result table just requires you to specify the name of the appropriate column, with the DESCending option if you require it.

Example:

```
SELECT * FROM salesmen
        ORDER BY qltarget DESC;
```

to show all salesmen with their targets, highest target first.

Result table:

Empno	Surname	Qltarget	Region
50005	James	60000	East
10001	Smith	50000	East
30003	Adams	50000	South
20002	Brown	40000	East
40004	Jones	25000	West

The command:

```
SELECT surname, qltarget FROM salesmen
        WHERE region = 'West'
        ORDER BY qltarget;
```

will show all salesmen in West Region in ascending order of target.

You do not have to include in the SELECT statement the column which you want to ORDER BY. So you could say:

```
SELECT surname FROM salesmen
        ORDER BY qltarget;
```

However, in practice you will find that it usually makes more sense to include it.

5.5.2 *Ordering by calculated or 'function' columns*

If you include a calculation in your SELECT column list, then you may well want to sort the result table on the outcome of this calculation.

However, SQL does not allow you to repeat the calculation in the ORDER BY clause. So it is wrong to say:

```
SELECT surname, q1target+q2target FROM salesmen
    ORDER BY q1target+q2target;              **ILLEGAL**
```

Instead you must refer to the column by its column number. The result table columns are numbered from 1 in the sequence in which you specify them. Thus, in the example above, 'surname' is column 1, and 'q1target+q2target' is column 2.

(This restriction also applies to the aggregate functions SUM, MIN, MAX etc. However, these functions only return a single row, and are therefore only subject to ORDER BY when used with the GROUP BY clause. We will be dealing with this in chapter 6.)

To order the result table on the target calculation, you would say:

```
SELECT surname, q1target+q2target FROM salesmen
    ORDER BY 2;
```

Although it is perfectly legal to use column numbers in *any* ORDER BY clause, your intentions are clearer if you use the column name. So, although you would get the same results from:

```
SELECT surname,empno FROM salesmen
    ORDER BY 2;
```

and

```
SELECT surname,empno FROM salesmen
    ORDER BY empno;
```

the second phrasing is clearer, and therefore to be preferred.

5.5.3 *Ordering by multiple columns*

If more than one row has the same value in the ORDER BY column, then although that group of rows will appear together in the sorted result table, the rows in the group will appear in no particular order. Indeed, you cannot even guarantee that the rows in the group will appear in the same order if you repeat an identical query several times! If you expect this situation to occur with the 'main' column of the ORDER BY, and if the consistent ordering of grouped rows is important to you, then you can specify a second (and third, fourth etc if necessary) column to ORDER BY. Columns are separated by commas. For example:

```
SELECT empno,qltarget FROM salesmen
    ORDER BY qltarget,empno;
```

When more than one column appears in the ORDER BY clause, groups of rows with the same column value are sorted on the basis of their value in the second column. If there is more than one row with identical values in the first and second ORDER BY columns, then this group is sorted on the third ORDER BY column, and so on.

Example:
Take the following 5 entries from the salesmen table.

Empno	qltarget
10003	50000
20001	45000
20003	50000
20002	75000
10002	50000

Ordering the table on qltarget with:

```
SELECT empno,qltarget FROM salesmen
    ORDER BY qltarget;
```

will produce

Empno	qltarget
20001	45000
10003	50000
20003	50000
10002	50000
20002	75000

All rows with the same 'qltarget' value are grouped together, but in an undefined order. Including a second column – empno – will show the group sorted into employee number order.

```
SELECT empno,qltarget FROM salesmen
    ORDER BY qltarget,empno;
```

Here is the new result table:

Empno	qltarget
20001	45000
10002	50000
10003	50000
20003	50000
20002	75000

Using DESC in a multiple column list

Any of the columns in the ORDER BY clause can take the DESCending option. To see the above table with employee numbers in descending order, say:

```
SELECT empno,qltarget FROM salesmen
    ORDER BY qltarget,empno DESC;
```

Here is the result table:

Empno	qltarget
20001	45000
20003	50000
10003	50000
10002	50000
20002	75000

Summary

In this chapter you were introduced to the full range of options available on SQL's SELECT command. Some of the clauses have been given in-depth treatment; others have just been touched upon.

In chapter 6 we will cover the rest of the SELECT options.

6 *More about SELECT*

Overview

This chapter carries on examining the options available with the SELECT command. Most important, you will see how to use joins to use SELECT options with multiple tables. You will also learn how to summarise row details by groups, and carry out more complex subqueries.

Major commands and topics covered

SELECT..GROUP BY   Multiple tables and joins
UNION   Advanced subqueries

6.1 Introduction

In this chapter we will continue with our discussion of the SELECT command. First we will finish working through the SELECT clauses that were not covered in detail in the last chapter – GROUP BY and UNION. Then we will look at the whole area of retrieving data from more than one table with a single SELECT statement. We will also discuss subqueries in more detail, showing you how to deal with a subquery that returns a set of values rather than a single item.

6.2 GROUP BY columnlist

One of things that you will often want to do is to create summaries of your data. For example, you might want to see the total target figures for each of the four sales regions in the example system, or to see the total value of orders placed by each customer.

    SQL uses the GROUP BY clause to accomplish this kind of task.

    GROUP BY produces a result table which contains just *one* row for every 'group' of rows in the base table that contain the same value in the column(s) specified in the GROUP BY clause.

6.2.1 Restrictions on SELECT columnlist with GROUP BY

Because GROUP BY acts by summarising column values, it forces restrictions on the columns which can be chosen for display in 'SELECT columnlist'. You can say:

```
SELECT region FROM salesmen
    GROUP BY region;
```

(to show a list of the different regions). In the example system we would see:

```
Region
------
North
South
East
West
```

But you cannot say:

```
SELECT surname,region FROM salesmen
    GROUP BY region;                           ** ILLEGAL **
```

SQL cannot produce a list of regions which *also* summarises salesmen's names!

6.2.2 Rule for including columns in SELECT columnlist

The rule for deciding which columns can appear in the SELECT columnlist is that you can only include:

- the column or combination of columns which form the basis for the grouping, and/or
- an aggregate function (SUM, COUNT etc)

6.2.3 Aggregate functions with GROUP BY

In the previous chapter we saw how the aggregate functions can be applied over the entire table. Used in exactly the same way, they become even more informative when in conjunction with a GROUP BY clause. For example:

```
SELECT region,SUM(q1target) FROM salesmen
    GROUP BY region;
```

gives the result table like:

```
Region      Sum(qltarget)
-----------------------
North          790000
South          999999
East           987654
West           500000
```

To expand the query to also show the number of salesmen in each region, and their average target, just say:

```
SELECT region, SUM(qltarget), COUNT(*), AVG(qltarget)
```

to give

```
Region      Sum(qltarget)  COUNT(*)  AVG(qltarget)
--------------------------------------------------
North          790000         10         79000
South          999999         25         39999
East           987654         20         49382
West           500000         10         50000
```

You cannot use an aggregate function in the GROUP BY clause itself. So you cannot say something like:

```
SELECT region FROM salesmen
    GROUP BY SUM(qltarget);              ** ILLEGAL **
```

6.2.4 Columns in GROUP BY that do not appear in SELECT columnlist

You can include a column in the GROUP BY clause that does not appear in the SELECT columnlist, although in most cases it does not make much sense to do so. You could say:

```
SELECT SUM(qltarget), COUNT(*), AVG(qltarget) FROM salesmen
    GROUP BY region;
```

to give the result table

```
Sum(qltarget)  COUNT(*)  AVG(qltarget)
--------------------------------------------------
   790000         10         79000
   999999         25         39999
   987654         20         49382
   500000         10         50000
```

But, as you can see, the result table is meaningless because it does not show *what* these figures are talking about. You need to include 'region' in the SELECT columnlist, as we did in the example in 6.2.3.

6.2.5 *Multiple columns in GROUP BY*

You can group rows based on their values in more than one column. In this case, all rows with identical values in all the columns specified will form one group.

For example, the command:

```
SELECT region, qltarget, COUNT(*) FROM salesmen
    GROUP BY region,qltarget;
```

will show one row for each different target within a region, together with the number of salesmen on this target.

Region	qltarget	COUNT(*)
North	50000	5
North	75000	5
South	50000	6
South	75000	10
South	85000	9
East	25000	10
West	50000	7
West	55000	3

Since rows are grouped on the basis of identical values in *all* specified columns, the order in which you specify the columns makes no difference to the result. So the command:

```
SELECT region, qltarget, COUNT(*) FROM salesmen
    GROUP BY qltarget,region;
```

will produce exactly the same result table as the previous example.

Note that this is completely different from what happens in the ORDER BY clause where changing the order of specified columns would produce a totally different result.

6.2.6 *Using GROUP BY with WHERE and ORDER BY*

Both these clauses work in their 'normal' manner when used in conjunction with a GROUP BY. So

```
SELECT region,SUM(q1target) FROM salesmen
    GROUP BY region
    ORDER BY region;
```

will show the four regions in alphabetical order.

```
Region      SUM(q1target)
-----------------------
East        987654
North       790000
South       999999
West        500000
```

```
SELECT region,SUM(q1target) FROM salesmen
    WHERE region <> 'East'
    GROUP BY region
    ORDER BY region;
```

will give us the same table as above, *without* a row for 'East' region.

```
Region      SUM(q1target)
-----------------------
North       790000
South       999999
West        500000
```

6.3 HAVING condition

HAVING is used as a qualifier on the GROUP BY clause. As we said in chapter 5, it is 'a WHERE clause for groups'. GROUP BY produces an 'intermediate' result table, which HAVING then checks to see which rows satisfy the condition. Those that do not are excluded from the final result table.

For example, if you wanted to perform a query showing the total Quarter 1 targets per region, *but only* for those regions where the total comes to more than 900000, you would say:

```
SELECT region,SUM(q1target) FROM salesmen
    GROUP BY region
    HAVING SUM(q1target) > 700000;
```

and get the result table

```
Region          SUM(qltarget)
-----------------------
East            987654
South           999999
```

It would be impossible to use WHERE to obtain the same result, because *a WHERE condition can never contain aggregate functions*. SQL will reject any attempt to say something like:

```
SELECT region,SUM(qltarget) FROM salesmen
    WHERE SUM(qltarget) > 900000          ** ILLEGAL **
    GROUP BY region;
```

6.4 UNION..SELECT statement

6.4.1 How UNION works

UNION allows you to use a single SQL statement to perform more than one separate query on base tables and then combine the results into a single result table. For example, if we wanted to see all salesmen in 'East' region, and also all salesmen with a target of more than 100000, we could say:

```
SELECT empno,surname,qltarget FROM salesmen
    WHERE region = 'East'
    UNION
    SELECT empno,surname,qltarget FROM salesmen
        WHERE qltarget > 100000;
```

In the result table, the rows retrieved by the first SELECT come before the rows retrieved by the second SELECT. If you want to change the order, use ORDER BY to apply to the whole result table (*not* to each separate SELECT). So:

```
SELECT empno,surname,qltarget FROM salesmen
    WHERE region = 'East'
    UNION
    SELECT empno,surname,qltarget FROM salesmen
        WHERE qltarget > 100000
    ORDER BY empno;
```

will produce the same rows in employee number sequence.

6.4.2 UNION of different tables

In 6.4.1, we carried out two SELECTs on the same table. But you can also use UNION to combine rows from different tables. So you could say:

```
SELECT empno,surname,address FROM salesmen
       WHERE region = 'East'
       UNION
       SELECT empno,surname,address FROM managers
              WHERE region = 'East';
```

to see the combined rows of Managers and Salesmen who work for 'East' region.

6.4.3 Restrictions on use of UNION

The columns given in each SELECT columnlist must be identical, both in name and in specification (i.e. data type and length).

You must specify the same columns in each SELECT statement.

So you could not create a result table containing three columns 'Empno' and 'Surname' (from 'salesmen') plus 'Title' (from 'managers') with a command like:

```
SELECT empno,surname FROM salesmen
UNION                                    ** ILLEGAL **
SELECT empno,surname,title FROM managers;
```

Also, if the 'managers' table had defined 'surname' as being 30 characters wide, as opposed to the 'salesmen' table's 20, then the next query will fail:

```
SELECT empno,surname FROM salesmen
UNION
SELECT empno,salesmen FROM managers;
```

6.4.4 UNION versus WHERE..OR..

If you want to combine rows from two different tables, then you *have* to use UNION. But if you use UNION in two SELECTs from the same table, then in most cases you could equally well use a WHERE..OR.. condition instead.

So to obtain the same result table as in 6.4.1 in another way, we could have said:

```
SELECT empno,surname,qltarget FROM salesmen
       WHERE region = 'East'
              OR qltarget > 100000;
```

6.4.4.1 How UNION can be different from WHERE..OR..
Using UNION in two SELECTs from the same table usually gives identical results to using an OR condition in a WHERE clause.

However, the ANSI standard uses opposite conventions for the defaults for DISTINCT and ALL in SELECT and UNION clauses, which can make a considerable difference to the result tables produced by the two different methods. SELECT assumes a default of ALL; UNION assumes a default of DISTINCT. In other words, all duplicate rows are eliminated in a UNION statement unless you specifically demand ALL rows, whereas in a WHERE..OR.. condition they would automatically be retained. So the statement:

```
SELECT surname FROM salesmen
UNION
SELECT surname FROM salesmen;
```

will produce exactly the same result table as

```
SELECT surname FROM salesmen;
```

But saying

```
SELECT surname FROM salesmen
UNION ALL
SELECT surname FROM salesmen;
```

will 'double up' the result table, with each salesman's name appearing twice.

It is unlikely that you would ever want to do this – but it is useful to know what possibilities exist!

6.5 Multiple Tables in SELECTs

6.5.1 Introduction

In all our discussions about SELECT so far, we have considered the effect of SELECT on a single table. This approach made it easier for you to absorb the intricacies of the various SELECT clauses. However, you can equally well use SELECT to extract information from more than one table. Relational theory calls this type of operation a **join**.

Let us see how you can adapt the SELECTs that you already know about to work with multiple tables.

6.5.2 SELECTing columns from several tables

To turn a single-table query into a join, you have to tell SQL unambiguously what columns you want from which tables, and how to link the various tables together.

In other words, you need to add:

- the *names of all tables* from which data is required (in the FROM clause)
- the *names of all columns* involved from all tables
- a *table prefix* for any columns with the same name in more than one table
- the *basis for the join* (in a WHERE clause)

We will take some examples from the 'salesmen' and 'contracts' tables. To start with, let us assume that we have only two salesmen, and only three contracts.

Example base tables

```
        salesmen                    contracts

empno surname           empno custname          amount
-----------------       ------------------------------
10001 Smith             20002 Thames Bros.       50000
20002 Jones             10001 Hi Markets         25000
                        10001 Astra & Co         10000
```

To show the employee number and surname of every salesman, together with the customer name and amount for all their contracts (one row per contract), you would say:

```
SELECT empno,surname,custname,amount
    FROM salesmen,contracts
    WHERE salesmen.empno = contracts.empno;
```

The result table would show:

```
empno surname     custname         amount
-----------------------------------------
20002 Jones       Thames Bros.      50000
10001 Smith       Hi Markets        25000
10001 Smith       Astra & Co        10000
```

As you see, a join is not difficult to do! We simply specified:

The names of all tables involved

```
..FROM salesmen,contracts
```

The FROM clause gives a comma-separated list of tables which SQL has to interrogate.

The names of all columns involved

```
SELECT empno,surname,custname,amount..
```

The SELECT columnlist just specifies all column names in the order that you want them. You do not have to include either of the columns on which the tables are joined (in our case, the 'empno' columns), although in practice you will find that it probably makes sense to include at least one.

A table prefix where column names are the same in both tables

```
..WHERE salesmen.empno = contracts.empno
```

If columns in both tables have the same name, then you must specify in the query which table you intend to refer to. Prefix the column name with the table name followed by a full stop.

It is always possible to give a column name a table prefix, whether it is required or not. So we could quite validly have given the SELECT command:

```
SELECT salesman.empno,salesmen.surname,
       contracts.custname,contracts.amount
       FROM salesmen,contracts
       WHERE salesmen.empno = contracts.empno;
```

You should do this if it makes your SELECT command clearer to understand.

You can also set up an alias for a table name. See section 6.6.3 for a full explanation.

The basis for the join

```
..WHERE salesmen.empno = contracts.empno
```

If two tables are to be joined together, they *must* both have a 'cross-reference' column which contains a value that is the same in both tables. If the two tables have nothing in common, then it will be impossible to link them together.

The columns do not have to have the same name, but they must have the same column specification. So, provided that employee numbers in the 'contracts' table are defined as CHAR(5), as in 'salesmen', then it would not matter if the column name was 'empnum' rather than 'empno'.

You do not have to define formally the basis of the join as a permanent relationship (unlike dBASE III/IV's SET RELATION command). Simply giving the cross-reference column in the WHERE clause is sufficient.

The figure below shows conceptually what SQL does.

```
         salesmen        |                contracts

   empno surname         |    empno custname        amount
   -----------------     |    ------------------------------
   10001 Smith           |    20002 Thames Bros.     50000
   20002 Jones           |    10001 Hi Markets       25000
                         ¦    10001 Astra & Co       10000
```

SQL works out that 'empno' and 'surname' come from the 'salesmen' table, and that 'custname' and 'amount' come from 'contracts'. It then forms the links between the two tables to extract the 'matching' rows.

6.5.3 Setting up an alias for a table

As you can see from the above examples, you can soon end up with a long SELECT statement full of table prefixes. You can save yourself typing, whilst still retaining the clarity that table prefixes give your statements, by defining another name – an alias – by which you can refer to the table.

To define an alias, follow the table name in the FROM clause with a space, and then the alias. For example:

```
..FROM salesmen s, contracts c
```

Although an alias can be any valid table name, it makes sense to set up a short (although still meaningful) name.

If an alias has been defined, then you *must* use the alias rather than the table name throughout the whole SELECT statement. So it is valid to say:

```
SELECT s.empno,s.surname,c.custname,c.amount
       FROM salesmen s, contracts c
       WHERE s.empno = c.empno;
```

But you could *not* say:

```
SELECT salesmen.empno,salesmen.surname,
       contracts.custname,contracts.amount
       FROM salesmen s, contracts c
       WHERE s.empno = c.empno;          ** ILLEGAL **
```

6.5.4 Different types of joins

There are several different types of join available within SQL. It is fairly common for manuals to refer to them by the names by which they are known in the relational model. Here is an explanation of the various types.

6.5.4.1 *General join*

In a general join, all columns in the WHERE clause also appear in the SELECT columnlist. This is usually achieved by using the * (all columns) with SELECT. So:

```
SELECT * FROM salesmen,contracts
      WHERE salesmen.empno = contracts.empno;
```

is a general join.

6.5.4.2 *Natural join*

A natural join is a join where fewer join columns appear in the SELECT columnlist than in the WHERE clause. As we said above, you do not have to include all, or indeed any, of the WHERE columns in the result table. It is perfectly valid to produce natural joins with:

```
SELECT surname,amount FROM salesmen,contracts
      WHERE salesmen.empno = contracts.empno;
```

(no 'join' columns in the SELECT list).

and

```
SELECT empno,surname,amount FROM salesmen,contracts
      WHERE salesmen.empno = contracts.empno;
```

(one 'join' column in the SELECT list).

6.5.4.3 *Equi-join*

An equi-join is one where the tables are linked by a condition of equality – in other words, the = sign. Both general and natural joins can also be equi-joins, as you can see from the examples above.

6.5.4.4 *Non-equi-join*

Not surprisingly, a non-equi-join is one where tables are linked by a condition of inequality – for example, <>, <, or >. Again, both general and natural joins can be non-equi-joins. In practice, non-equi-joins are not very common.

6.5.4.5 *Inner and outer joins*

The distinctions between the various joins described above may seem rather esoteric. However, the distinction between an inner and an outer join has direct influence on the results of a SELECT query! What is more, ANSI SQL supports the inner join, but not the outer join.

Inner joins

Normally, if a row in one of the tables to be joined has no matching value in the other table, then no corresponding row will appear in the 'joined' result table.

Let us illustrate this with an example. First we will add a new salesman, James Brown, to the 'salesmen' table, with an employee number '10003'. Since he is new, he has not sold anything yet, so he has no entries in the 'contracts' table. The base 'salesmen' and 'contracts' tables now contain:

```
         salesmen                        contracts

    empno surname        empno custname           amount
    -----------------    -------------------------------
    10001 Smith          20002 Thames Bros.        50000
    20002 Jones          10001 Hi Markets          25000
    10003 Brown          10001 Astra & Co          10000
```

The join statement:

```
    SELECT salesmen.empno,surname,custname,amount
        FROM salesmen,contracts
        WHERE salesmen.empno = contracts.empno;
```

will still give

```
    empno surname     custname          amount
    ------------------------------------------
    20002 Jones       Thames Bros.      50000
    10001 Smith       Hi Markets        25000
    10001 Smith       Astra & Co        10000
```

exactly as it did before employee number '10003' had been added to the table! Because there is no corresponding entry for '10003' in 'contracts', the inner join rule cannot allow this employee to appear at all.

Outer joins

Obviously, it can be useful to see rows for which there is no matching entry in another table – for example, all salesmen who have not sold anything.

Some SQL implementations – for example, Oracle and Informix – support the outer join to allow just that facility.

Such SQLs require you to state specifically that a particular join is an outer join. Inner joins are always the default. Oracle uses a (+) to signal an outer join; Informix uses OUTER. For example, in Oracle you would say

```
SELECT salesmen.empno,surname
     FROM salesmen,contracts
     WHERE salesmen.empno = contracts.empno (+);
```

to give the result table:

```
empno surname
----- -------
10003 Brown
```

6.5.4.6 Subqueries instead of outer joins

If your version of SQL does not support outer joins, you can still get the required result by using a **subquery** instead. (See section 6.6 for further discussion of subqueries.) To get the same result as the example above, you could say:

```
SELECT empno,surname FROM salesmen
     WHERE empno NOT IN
     (SELECT empno FROM contracts);
```

Although this is not in itself any more complicated than using a join, it makes yet another different thing to learn!

6.6 More on subqueries

6.6.1 Introduction

In chapter 5, we looked at subqueries returning a single value, used on the same table as the main SELECT. For example:

```
SELECT empno,surname FROM salesmen
     WHERE q1target >
     (SELECT AVG(q1target) FROM salesmen);
```

to show all salesmen whose target is greater than the average.

We used one of the aggregate functions to make sure that the subquery returned a single value, and used a simple arithmetic operator for the comparison.

We will now look at using subqueries on multiple tables, and at subqueries which return a set of values.

6.6.2 Subqueries on multiple tables

You can apply a subquery to a table other than that on which the main SELECT is being performed. For example, you might want to find all salesmen whose Quarter 1 target is greater than the maximum contract value in the contracts table. You could achieve this with:

```
SELECT empno,surname FROM salesmen
    WHERE q1target >
    (SELECT MAX(amount) FROM contracts);
```

6.6.3 Subqueries returning a set of values

You will find that you often need to perform a query which checks a column value against a *set*, or *list*, of other values (which may be in either the same table or in a different table from the main SELECT). For example, you might want to see:

- salesmen who have no entry in the contracts table
- salesmen whose target is different from any target for anyone in East Region

To accomplish such tasks, you need to use a different set of WHERE operators. Provided for this purpose are:

```
IN
NOT IN
EXISTS
NOT EXISTS
ANY
ALL
```

6.6.3.1 IN and NOT IN

This operation is similar in concept to the IN (list) we discussed in section 5.4.5. The only difference is that for IN (list) *the user* has to specify the list of values for comparison; in a subquery SQL works out the list for itself.

So, to see all salesmen in North, South and West regions whose target is the same as any target for anyone in East region, you would say:

```
SELECT empno,surname FROM salesmen
    WHERE q1target IN
    (SELECT q1target FROM salesmen
        WHERE region = 'East')
    AND region <> 'East';
```

SQL first evaluates the subquery to produce an 'internal' list of all the

Quarter 1 targets for everyone in East Region. It then compares each target in the base table against this list. If a target appears in the list, then that row is passed to the 'intermediate' result table. This result table is then checked in the normal way to remove rows not in East Region.

You can reverse the effect of IN by preceding it with NOT. Repeating the query above with NOT IN instead of IN will show you everyone in North, South and West regions whose target is different from any target in the 'internal' list generated by the subquery.

6.6.3.2 ANY

ANY is used in conjunction with the arithmetic operators to check a column value as being equal to, greater than or less than *any* value in the list generated by the subquery.

You can use ANY preceded by any arithmetic operator. For example:

```
>ANY          (greater than any..)
=ANY          (equal to any..)
<=ANY         (less than or equal to any..)
```

Using **=ANY** is equivalent to using **IN**. The query in 6.6.3.1 could equally well have been expressed as:

```
SELECT empno,surname FROM salesmen
     WHERE q1target =ANY
     (SELECT q1target FROM salesmen
           WHERE region = 'East')
     AND region <> 'East';
```

You can use ANY in ways which might not seem obvious at first glance. For instance, if you want to see all salesmen except those on the lowest target figure, you could say

```
SELECT empno,surname FROM salesmen
     WHERE q1target > ANY
     (SELECT q1target FROM salesmen);
```

As a result of the subquery, SQL generates an 'internal' list of all Quarter 1 target figures. It then checks each target figure in the base table to see if it is larger than any of the values in the internal table. Only the lowest target figures are **equal to** rather than **greater than** any other values in the internal list, and so all rows except these are passed to the final result table.

You will probably agree that this is *not* intuitively obvious! For this reason, you will often be better off avoiding the use of ANY, and rephrasing the query. Luckily this is usually quite easy to do. We could produce the same result table of all salesmen not on the lowest target figure by giving the much clearer statement:

```
SELECT empno,surname FROM salesmen
     WHERE q1target <>
     (SELECT MIN(q1target) FROM salesmen);
```

6.6.3.3 ALL

ALL is used in a similar way to ANY – i.e. with the arithmetic operators. However, in an ALL condition, the WHERE column value has to be greater than/less than etc *all* the values generated by the subquery.

For this reason, it does not make sense to use ALL with the equals sign, as in =**ALL**. Such a condition could only evaluate as TRUE if all the values in the 'internal' subquery list were identical.

To see all salesmen on the lowest Quarter 1 target level you could say:

```
SELECT empno,surname FROM salesmen
     WHERE q1target <= ALL
     (SELECT q1target FROM salesmen);
```

Again, the subquery generates an internal list of all Quarter 1 target values. It then checks each base table target figure against the entire list to eliminate all those where the target is higher than *any* value in the list. Only the lowest target figures do not come into this category, so only those salesmen on the lowest target value are passed to the final result table.

Just as with ANY, this evaluation is certainly not obvious at first sight. Again, you should rephrase the query more clearly if possible. We could produce the same result with the much simpler:

```
SELECT empno,surname FROM salesmen
     WHERE q1target =
     (SELECT MIN(q1target) FROM salesmen);
```

6.6.3.4 EXISTS and NOT EXISTS

EXISTS checks for each row in the base table whether any rows at all satisfy the condition in the subquery. If any do, then EXISTS is TRUE.

EXISTS is the only subquery operator which allows you to specify more than one column in the subquery SELECT. This is because an EXISTS clause does not check a particular column value (as every other subquery does); it merely produces a TRUE/FALSE result. In fact, it is easiest to use the * (all columns) in an EXISTS clause.

EXISTS is almost always used to check whether or not a particular value occurs in a different table from that used in the main SELECT. We could use EXISTS as a way to find out which salesmen have entries in the contracts table:

```
SELECT empno,name FROM salesmen
    WHERE EXISTS
    (SELECT * FROM contracts
        WHERE salesmen.empno = contracts.empno);
```

To see salesmen who have not made any sales, you could replace EXISTS with NOT EXISTS:

```
SELECT empno,name FROM salesmen
    WHERE NOT EXISTS
    (SELECT * FROM contracts
        WHERE salesmen.empno = contracts.empno);
```

(See section 6.5.4.5 for another way of getting the same result.)

You can always replace an ANY or an ALL condition with an appropriate EXISTS/NOT EXISTS one.

Summary

You have now covered all the major elements of the SELECT statement. As you now realise, SELECT is really the most important command in an SQL system; certainly it is the one which most users will use for 90% of their work.

In the next chapter we will look at how the data that SELECT uses actually gets into the tables in the first place!

7 *Updating the Database*

Overview

In this chapter we will discuss the various ways of updating tables. You will learn the commands to enter new rows, alter existing data items, delete rows – and recover from mistakes! We will also discuss ways of transferring data from one table to another, and how to 'import' data from a non-SQL file into an SQL table.

Commands and major topics covered

INSERT..VALUES	INPUT
INSERT INTO..	COMMIT
UPDATE..SET	ROLLBACK
DELETE FROM	Import/Export commands

7.1 Introduction

So far we have spent a lot of time looking at the ways of retrieving data from existing tables. But we have only given a cursory glance to the ways in which that data gets into the tables in the first place (see section 3.3.2 for a short discussion of INSERT).

It made sense to discuss the SELECT command before the various data input and editing commands, because the UPDATE and DELETE commands rely heavily on knowledge of the WHERE clauses used in SELECT. You often need to perform tasks such as:

- increase all East Region targets by 10%
- change John Smith's home phone number
- delete all salesmen in North Region

and so on. All these would require a condition to force the update to apply only to the required set of rows.

SQL provides various ways of updating tables. The commands used vary with the kind of update that you want to perform. Naturally, they also vary to some extent between implementations. This is particularly true in the area of transfer of data to and from non-SQL files and SQL tables (for example, transferring rows from a dBASE III database into an Oracle table, or from Oracle to Lotus 1–2–3). The ANSI standard does not lay down any rules for such commands. We will cover them here because it is an area which is becoming more and more important as SQL systems proliferate on PC-based systems.

The various types of update that can be applied to the database are:

- interactively adding a completely new row (all columns)
- interactively adding a completely new row (some columns only)
- changing some or all column entries for one or more rows
- deleting one or more rows
- transferring one or more rows from one table to another
- creating new rows by 'importing' data from a non-SQL table

7.2 Interactively adding new rows – INSERT (and INPUT)

7.2.1 Syntax of INSERT

'Interactively' is used here to highlight the difference in updating techniques between the user *typing in* one or more new rows (interactive), and a '*block*' transfer of rows from one table (or non-SQL file) to another.

We are dealing here with the simple situation where the user needs to perform a task such as:

- add a new salesman to the 'salesman' table
- add a new contract for a salesman

The SQL command to achieve this is:

```
INSERT INTO tablename (columnlist) VALUES
        (valuelist);
```

This allows you to enter one new row, with values input either into all columns in the table, or into specified columns only.

The row that you INSERTed will normally appear as the last row of the table. However, since base tables are, by definition, unordered, you should not rely on it appearing in any particular position. Use ORDER BY with your SELECT command if the order of rows is important to you.

Some SQLs (for example, Informix) also provide a non-standard command like:

```
INPUT (columnlist)
                (row 1 values
                row 2 values
                etc..);
```

which allows you to enter column values into several new rows with a single command. We will not go into it in detail here. However, as always, you should be aware that your particular SQL implementation may contain features that are not in the ANSI standard, but which you may find very useful! (Just to confuse matters, Oracle uses a command 'INPUT' as part of the process of adding to and editing commands that you previously typed in!)

7.2.2 Adding a new row – data into all columns

This is the simplest form of the INSERT command. Simply specify the table to be updated, and then list the values for each column. You *must* enter a value for every column in the table. Values are assigned to columns on a 'left-to-right' basis.

We will create a small version of the 'salesmen' table to illustrate the updating commands. Here is the CREATE command to set up 'salesmen';

```
CREATE TABLE salesmen
        (empno      CHAR(5),
        surname    CHAR(20),
        region     CHAR(5),
        qltarget   NUMBER(8,2)
        datejoined DATE);
```

To insert a new row, you would say:

```
INSERT INTO salesmen VALUES
        ('40004',
        'Marks',
        'North',
        75000
        TO_DATE('1-JAN-87'));
```

(Remember that the 'date' data type is not standard ANSI SQL, and that although most SQLs implement it, they will often require a function to convert character input to date format.)

7.2.3 *Adding a new row – data into selected columns*

You can use INSERT VALUES to specify exactly which columns you want to input data for. Values are then assigned on a 'left-to-right' basis into the columns you specify. For example, you may want to enter a row for which you do not yet know the target figure or the region. To do so, just say:

```
INSERT INTO salesmen (empno,surname,datejoined) VALUES
        ('40004',
        'Marks',
        TO_DATE('1-JAN-87'));
```

7.2.4 *Restrictions on INSERT VALUES*

1. Integrity constraints

The row that you INSERT must obviously satisfy any integrity constraints defined during CREATE TABLE – for example, some columns may have been specified as NOT NULL or NOT NULL UNIQUE. (See chapter 4 for a discussion of the CREATE TABLE command.) All data entered must naturally be of the right type and length for that column.

2. Only one table at a time

INSERT can operate on only one table. So this attempt to enter both a new salesman and his first contract is illegal.

```
INSERT INTO salesmen (empno,surname),        ** ILLEGAL **
        contracts (empno,amount)
VALUES ('40004','Marks','40004',10000);
```

You will have to perform two separate INSERTs to get the result that you require.

7.3 **Changing existing data – UPDATE**

7.3.1 *Rules for using UPDATE*

To edit data items that are already in the table, you need to use the SQL command UPDATE. This takes the form:

```
UPDATE tablename
        SET columnname = newvalue
        (WHERE condition);
```

This allows you to update one or more columns for all rows, or for selected rows in the table.

The new value for the column can be a constant (e.g. 100000 or 'South'), a calculation (e.g. q1target * 1.1), or a value from another column (setting q1target equal to q2target). Naturally, the new value must conform to the column specifications defined when the table was CREATEd.

If no WHERE clause is given, then the UPDATE will be applied to all rows. In a WHERE clause, you can use any of the condition operators you learned about for SELECT. You can also use subqueries. See chapters 5 and 6 for more information on WHERE clauses.

You can specify several columns to be updated in the same UPDATE statement. Simply repeat the format 'columnname = newvalue' as many times as necessary. Separate each column update with a comma.

UPDATEs are applied row by row, starting from the top of the table.

7.3.2 *Examples of UPDATE*

Here are some examples of UPDATEs.

Let us assume that the 'salesmen' table has in it the following rows:

Empno	Surname	Region	Q1target	Datejoined
10001	Smith	East	50000	7-OCT-85
30003	Jones	West	99000	23-JAN-89
20002	Adams	East	40000	13-FEB-82
40004	Marks	South	60000	01-JAN-87

Examples of single-column updates
You could edit the original table to increase all targets by 10% with:

```
UPDATE salesmen                          Calculation,
     SET q1target = q1target*1.1;          all rows
```

You could increase the targets for all salesmen in East Region by adding a WHERE clause to the statement:

```
UPDATE salesmen                          Calculation,
     SET q1target = q1target*1.1           row subset
     WHERE region = 'East';
```

You could change all entries for 'East' to 'S.E' with:

```
UPDATE salesmen
     SET region = 'S.E.'                  Constant,
     WHERE region = 'East';                row subset
```

You could use a subquery to give employee number 10001 the same target as employee 20002:

```
UPDATE salesmen                              Column Value,
     SET qltarget =                           row subset
            (SELECT qltarget FROM salesmen
                 WHERE empno = '20002')
          WHERE empno = '10001';
```

And you could even use a subquery to give employee number 10001 the same target figure as the manager whose employee number is '90009' (from the 'managers' table):

```
UPDATE salesmen                              Column Value,
     SET qltarget =                           row subset
            (SELECT qltarget FROM managers
                 WHERE managerno = '90009')
          WHERE empno = '10001';
```

Examples of multiple-column updates
In all the above examples, you could have updated several columns in each row. For example, to increase the targets of salesmen in East Region by 10% *and* to change the name 'East' to 'S.E.', you would say:

```
UPDATE salesmen
     SET qltarget = qltarget*1.1,
         region = 'S.E.'
     WHERE region = 'East';
```

7.3.3 Restrictions on UPDATE

7.3.3.1 Only one table at a time
UPDATE cannot update more than one table at once. So a command which attempts to change employee number 10001's region to 'East', *and* the amount of his sale (in the contract table) to 7000:

```
UPDATE salesmen,contracts                    ** ILLEGAL **
     SET region = 'East',
         amount = 7000
     WHERE empno = '10001';
```

will fail.

To achieve the required result, you would have to perform two separate updates.

7.3.3.2 No 'self-referencing' of tables in WHERE subqueries

If an UPDATE includes a WHERE clause, and that WHERE clause itself includes a subquery, then the table being referenced in the subquery's FROM clause cannot be the same as the table being updated. In other words, the following UPDATE, which attempts to set to 90000 all targets smaller than the average, is illegal:

```
UPDATE salesmen                              ** ILLEGAL **
      SET qltarget = 90000
            WHERE qltarget <
                  (SELECT AVG(qltarget) FROM salesmen);
```

This is true for ANSI SQL and DB2. However, Oracle is quite happy to process such a 'self-referencing' statement correctly.

7.3.3.3 Problems with UNIQUE columns

You know from chapter 3 that a column can be defined as NOT NULL UNIQUE, or that a UNIQUE INDEX can be created on a column. This has the effect of stopping any one value from appearing more than once in the table. UPDATE can have problems when updating such a column, since as soon as SQL finds a violation of the UNIQUE property of the column, the UPDATE will stop.

Normally, of course, you *want* such violations to be stopped from getting into the table. So, if you attempt to add a row for employee number '10001', and there is already an entry for this salesman in the table, then the attempt will, correctly, be rejected.

But there are some circumstances where you would like UPDATE to temporarily ignore the UNIQUE constraint. Let us assume that you want to increase all the employee numbers by 1. (For the sake of simplicity, we will also assume that 'empno' was created as a NUMBER column, and that the current table holds the rows in the order 10001, 10002, 10003 etc.)

The command to achieve this operation would be:

```
UPDATE salesmen
      SET empno = empno+1;
```

However, as soon as UPDATE 'adds one to' the employee number in the first row, 10001 becomes 10002. This immediately violates the UNIQUE constraint; there is *already* an entry for 10002 in the table! And so the UPDATE fails.

There is no easy way round this problem. Unfortunately, you cannot tell SQL to 'temporarily ignore' the UNIQUE constraint. If the problem was caused by a UNIQUE INDEX, then you will have to delete the index (DROP INDEX), perform the UPDATE, and recreate the index afterwards.

If the UNIQUE was specified as part of the column definition, then you could either use ALTER COLUMN..MODIFY to remove the UNIQUE (but remember, this is not ANSI SQL, and not all SQLs support the MODIFY clause), or create a new table without the UNIQUE constraint and transfer over and UPDATE the data there. (See section 7.5 for a full discussion of this subject.)

7.4 Deleting rows – DELETE

7.4.1 How to use DELETE

The DELETE command can be used to delete one or more rows from a table.

It takes the form:

```
DELETE FROM tablename
      (WHERE condition);
```

As with UPDATE, the WHERE clause is optional, and can contain any conditions that you could use in a SELECT clause.

For example, to delete all salesmen in 'East' region, you would say:

```
DELETE FROM salesmen
      WHERE region = 'East';
```

To delete a single employee you might say:

```
DELETE FROM salesmen
      WHERE empno = '10001';
```

7.4.2 Deleting all rows

Beware! If you use DELETE with no WHERE clause, then all the rows in the table will be deleted. This is *very* easy to do by mistake! So:

```
DELETE FROM salesmen;
```

will instantly remove all rows from the table. The table structure will remain intact; this is *not* the same as DROP TABLE.

7.4.3 Restrictions on DELETE

DELETE, just like UPDATE, cannot contain a 'self-referencing' table in the WHERE clause. So an attempt to delete all rows where the target figure is less than the average target will fail:

```
DELETE FROM salesmen                          ** ILLEGAL **
       WHERE qltarget <
             SELECT AVG(qltarget) FROM salesmen;
```

As before, this is true for ANSI SQL and DB2, but not for Oracle.

7.5 Copying rows from one table to another – INSERT..SELECT..

7.5.1 How to use INSERT..SELECT

Another form of the INSERT command allows you to copy rows between tables. The command has the syntax:

```
INSERT INTO tablename (column list)
       SELECT statement;
```

The SELECT statement cannot include the GROUP BY, HAVING or ORDER BY clauses. But you can use the full range of WHERE operators, just as in a 'normal' SELECT. (Note that, as with UPDATE and DELETE, ANSI SQL does not permit a 'self-referencing' FROM clause. See section 7.3.3.2 for a description of the problem.)

You can choose to copy all columns (*), or a list of selected columns. In either case, the columns in your SELECT list will be assigned to the columns in the new table on a 'left-to-right' basis. You must include the correct number of columns 'on both sides' of the transfer; in other words, if the table that you are attempting to INSERT INTO has only two columns, then attempting to copy all columns from 'salesmen' will fail.

Naturally, data being copied over must be of the correct data type for each new table column. However, the columns do *not* have to be of the same width, or have the same names. For CHAR data, SQL will either 'pad out' a value with blanks, or truncate the entry to fit the new column width.

The rows that you SELECT for copying will be added to the new table. They do not replace any rows already there.

Here are some valid and invalid examples of INSERT..SELECT. First, let us create a new table with three columns:

```
CREATE TABLE newemp
       (empnum    CHAR(5),
        name      CHAR(15),
        qltarget  NUMBER (8,2));
```

7.5.2 *Valid INSERTs INTO newemp*

1. INSERT INTO newemp
        SELECT empno,surname,q1target FROM salesmen;

    This copies over the three specified columns from *all* rows.

2. INSERT INTO newemp
        SELECT empno,surname,q1target FROM salesmen
            WHERE region = 'East';

    This copies the three specified columns for salesmen in 'East' region only.

3. INSERT INTO newemp
        SELECT empno,surname,q1target*2 FROM salesmen;

    This copies the employee number, surname, and the target figure multiplied by 2, for all rows.

4. INSERT INTO newemp
        SELECT empno,surname,q1target FROM salesmen
            WHERE salesmen.empno NOT IN
                (SELECT empno FROM contracts);

    This copies those three columns for all salesmen with no entries in the 'contracts' table.

5. INSERT INTO newemp (empnum,q1target)
        SELECT empno,q1target FROM salesmen;

    This copies *only* the employee number and target, from all rows.

7.5.3 *Invalid INSERTs INTO newemp*

All the following INSERTs will fail. The reason for the failure is given below each statement.

1. INSERT INTO newemp
        SELECT * FROM salesmen;

    Fails because: The number of columns in 'salesmen' is greater than the number of columns in 'newemp'.

2. INSERT INTO newemp
        SELECT empno FROM salesmen;

    Fails because: There is more than one column in newemp.

3. INSERT INTO newemp
   SELECT empno,surname,q1target*100000 FROM salesmen;

   Fails because: The target figure is larger than the 6-integer width allowed by the column definition.

4. INSERT INTO newemp
   SELECT q1target,empno,surname FROM salesmen;

   Fails because: You cannot insert the contents of a NUMBER column ('q1target') into a CHAR column (empnum).

7.6 Using INSERT..SELECT to delete and alter columns

As we saw in chapter 3, ANSI SQL does not support a command to delete a column from a table. And the ALTER TABLE command only allows you to ADD a column rather than modifying the specification of an existing column (although some SQL implementations, such as Oracle, *do* provide a 'MODIFY' option).

You can carry out column deletion and modification (changing data types, column widths and names) by using the INSERT..SELECT command. The general 'steps' that you have to follow through are:

1. Create a new table (any name you like) containing the column definitions that you need.
2. Use INSERT INTO..SELECT.. to copy over the rows that you require from the old table (usually all rows).
3. SELECT from the System Catalog tables to find out what views and indexes depend on the original table.
4. DROP (or rename) the original table. All the indexes and views associated with it will also be dropped.
5. Rename the new table to have the same name as the original.

   (There is no ANSI SQL command 'RENAME', but most SQL's support such a command. If yours does not, then you will have to take the extra step of CREAT(E)ing another table with the correct new structure, calling it by the original name, and then doing another INSERT..SELECT to copy all rows and columns from the second table.)
6. Recreate any indexes or views which existed on the original table.

Do you really need a new table?

In some cases, you may find that you do not really need to create a new table. A VIEW may achieve the same end result with much less effort. If you simply want to show fewer columns, perhaps in a different order, with different column names, then a VIEW will probably do what you require. See the next chapter for a full discussion of what VIEWs can do for you.

7.7 'Undoing' your mistakes (COMMIT and ROLLBACK)

You are quite likely to make mistakes when updating the database. WHERE clauses are prone to error. It is easy to find that you have changed the target figure for *all* salesmen rather than just those in East Region or, even worse, that you have just deleted *all* rows in your table instead of just the one for employee number '10001'.

However, there is a way to recover from this apparently disastrous situation!

We mentioned in section 3.3.7 that transactions are not saved permanently into the database until the COMMIT WORK command has been issued. You can use the ROLLBACK WORK command to 'backtrack' from any wrongly entered update.

(Although the ANSI standard specifies the word 'WORK' as part of the COMMIT and ROLLBACK commands, most SQLs allow you to just say 'COMMIT' and 'ROLLBACK'.)

So, if you inadvertently deleted all rows with

```
DELETE FROM salesmen;
```

then you could simply say:

```
ROLLBACK WORK
```

to return the table to the state it was in at the time of the last COMMIT.

Of course, this may have the effect of removing other changes that you made which you *did* want to keep. You have to decide whether it is easier to ROLLBACK to a previous state, or 'manually' to undo the incorrect change.

The option to ROLLBACK will not be available to you if you have chosen to SET AUTOCOMMIT ON. In this case, all transactions are COMMITted automatically as soon as you enter them.

If you QUIT the SQL system, any unCOMMITted transactions are automatically COMMITted for you.

(Note that dBASE IV SQL does not support the COMMIT WORK command. It does support a BEGIN..END TRANSACTION block, and you can ROLLBACK to the beginning of the block at any time before the END TRANSACTION statement. In other circumstances, all changes to a dBASE IV SQL database are automatically COMMITted immediately.)

7.8 Importing and exporting data

You may be lucky enough to be able to be able to carry out all your work within a single SQL environment; for example, to manage to use Oracle for all database-management related tasks. But many users will find that the SQL product which they use quite happily for input and retrieval of data, cannot satisfy their other demands. This is especially true now that SQL systems are readily available on personal computers, whose users are accustomed to swapping data between packages. For example, they may want to:

- produce graphs from the data
- merge selected items into 'standard' letters produced by a word processing package
- copy data to a spreadsheet for more complex analysis and then bring it back into the SQL system.

Even the user who can happily achieve all that he wants to do within his SQL product, may find that he needs to use data produced by people who use different packages, or merely different SQL systems. Someone who uses a database under dBASE IV SQL may well need to exchange data with an Oracle user.

The various SQL suppliers recognise this requirement, and have provided for it in their own various ways. Since there is no ANSI specification for 'data interchange' commands, and since the IBM DB2 'standard' is weak in this respect, you will find that each supplier has its own way of importing and exporting data, with a greater or lesser degree of flexibilty.

The facilities offered range from dBASE IV SQL's very flexible (but PC-oriented) abilities to import and export everything from ASCII files through to Lotus 1–2–3 worksheets, through Oracle's ASCII to EBCDIC translator.

It is beyond the scope of this book to go through the operation of each system's 'conversion' commands. The important thing is that you should be aware that it is *possible* to import and export data from and to different systems.

For the four systems that we are considering in some detail in this book, here are the commands that you should look up:

Product	*Commands*
dBASE IV SQL	LOAD DATA (import)
	UNLOAD DATA (export)
Oracle	IMP and EXP
	The SQL*LOADER module
DB2	The LOAD utility
Informix	IMPORT

Summary

Now you know how to input data into a table, either interactively, by 'bulk' copying from another SQL table, or by importing rows from non-SQL files.

8 Creating and using views

Overview

In this chapter we will look at how views can be used to allow users easily to access different aspects of the database. We will see how to create views, what restrictions there are on using them, and discuss why you might want to use them at all!

Major commands and topics covered

CREATE VIEW
DROP VIEW

8.1 An overview of views

8.1.1 Why do you need views?

Most databases are likely to contain several tables, lots of columns, and even more rows. The sheer weight of information available can overwhelm the naive – and sometimes even the more experienced – user. Certainly, SQL provides a powerful tool in the SELECT command for structuring and retrieving exactly what data items are required at any one time – but most users do not want to spend their days formulating complex (and probably nearly identical) SELECT statements to extract what they want to see from the mass of data available. What is more, there may well be data items that some users should *not* be allowed to see. Should the accounts clerk be able to log in to SQL and look up the managing director's salary? The director would not think so! So we can see that this mass of information does not need to be, and in some cases cannot be allowed to be, available to all users at all times.

So it would be useful to have ways of:

– saving time when retrieving data

97

and/or
  –   restricting the data that users are allowed to access

SQL provides **VIEWS** to satisfy these needs.

8.1.2 What is a view?

The CREATE VIEW command allows the user to set up different 'views' of the database – different 'angles' from which to examine the data. Using the correct view will present the user immediately with exactly the data that he requires, without having to go through the tedious task of writing SELECT statements every time.

You can set up VIEWS which constrain their users to seeing:

  –   a subset of rows from one or more tables.
  –   a subset of columns from one or more tables.
  –   a subset of both rows and columns from one or more tables.

The diagram below shows you the concepts behind a view.

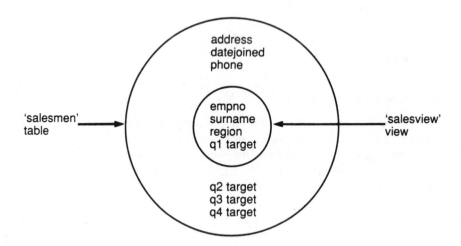

A VIEW is set up with a variation on the SELECT command. We will discuss the CREATE VIEW command in section 8.2; but here is an example of a simple CREATE VIEW just to show you the principle of how a view is formed.

```
CREATE VIEW eastsales AS
        SELECT empno,surname,qltarget FROM salesmen
        WHERE region = 'East';
```

Once the view called 'eastsales' has been created, then every time you want to see the employee number, surname and target of all salesmen in East Region all you need do is say:

```
SELECT * FROM eastsales;
```

There are some exceptions (see 8.5), but in general, any set of rows and columns that you could produce with a SELECT can form a VIEW. So you could easily set up different views to show their users:

- all salesmen in East Region
- all salesmen who have not sold anything yet
- the total contract amounts so far, grouped by region

and so on.

In most cases, a view appears to the user to be exactly like a base table. You can CREATE it, CREATE a SYNONYM for it, SELECT from it, UPDATE it and INSERT new rows into it (with certain restrictions; see 8.5) and DELETE it. You can grant different access privileges to different users, just as with a base table. (See 10.2.7 for a full discussion of privileges.)

However, a view is fundamentally different from a base table. A base table actually contains data. A VIEW is more like a result table which has been made permanently available for querying. But unlike a result table, a VIEW is dynamic. This means that if you change data in the base tables from which a VIEW is composed, then the data in the VIEW changes immediately to reflect the new base tables. Every time the view is used, SQL reinterprets the 'formula' which was used to create it and reproduces the latest version of the data. For this reason, a view is sometimes referred to as a **virtual table**.

8.2 Creating a view – CREATE VIEW

8.2.1 *The CREATE VIEW command*

The basic syntax of CREATE VIEW is:

```
CREATE VIEW viewname (column list) AS
     SELECT statement
          (WITH CHECK OPTION);
```

Both the column list and the **WITH CHECK OPTION** clause are optional.

Once a view has been created, its 'definition' (the SELECT formula which created it) is stored in the appropriate System Catalog table.

To create a view showing only salesmen in East Region, you could say:

```
CREATE VIEW eastsales AS
     SELECT empno,surname,address FROM salesmen
          WHERE region = 'East';
```

This creates the view 'eastsales', which contains three of the columns from 'salesmen' and only a subset of rows; i.e. those where region is 'East'.

Once this has been done, the user can access 'eastsales' just as if it was a base table. Every time he wants to see all salesmen in East Region, he can say:

```
SELECT * FROM eastsales;
```

rather than the longer

```
SELECT empno,surname,address from salesmen
     WHERE region = 'East';
```

In both cases, he would see the same display on the screen.

Avoiding the use of *

Although it is quite valid to specify the * (all columns) in the SELECT clause of a CREATE VIEW, doing so can lead to problems if the definition of the base table is altered. For example, you might create the view 'eastsales' with

```
CREATE VIEW eastsales AS
     SELECT * FROM salesmen
          WHERE region = 'East'
```

If you later add a new column to the salesmen table with:

```
ALTER TABLE salesmen
     ADD (postcode (CHAR 8));
```

most implementations of SQL, such as DB2 and Oracle, will spot an inconsistency between the original specification and the current base table, and any further operations referencing the view will fail. (This also holds true when deleting a column.)

For this reason it is always safer to specify all the individual column names in the SELECT clause, even though it may seem like a waste of time if you simply want to pick up all columns and use the names already defined in the base table.

If you do specify the column names individually, you are safeguarded against problems occurring when columns are added to the base table. However, you will still find similar problems if a base-table column is deleted, or has its name changed. Naturally, the view definition finds that an important part of its 'formula' is missing, and any further references to the view will fail.

8.2.2 *Row and column subsets*

As we mentioned above, views can consist of subsets of columns, rows or both columns and rows, from one or more tables. You use the SELECT..WHERE.. statement to specify which rows/columns are to be allowed into the view. Here are some examples of valid CREATE VIEWs:

```
CREATE VIEW largetarget AS          Row Subset, One Table
    SELECT * FROM salesmen
        WHERE q1target > 150000;

CREATE VIEW onlysurname AS          Column Subset, One Table
    SELECT surname FROM salesmen;

CREATE VIEW surtarget AS            Row and Column Subset,
    SELECT surname FROM salesmen            One Table
        WHERE q1target > 150000;

CREATE VIEW multirows AS                   Row Subset,
    SELECT * FROM salesmen s,contracts c    Two Tables
        WHERE s.empno = c.empno

CREATE VIEW multicols AS        Row and Column Subset
    SELECT s.empno,surname,amount          Two Tables
    FROM salesmen s, contracts c
        WHERE s.empno = c.empno;

CREATE VIEW region_group (region,total) AS    Grouped View
    SELECT region, SUM(q1target) FROM salesmen
        GROUP BY region;
```

As you can see, it appears that any SELECT statement which is valid when given as an ordinary data retrieval command, can also validly be used to create a VIEW. However, there are in fact quite a few restrictions on the SELECT statements which can be made. These are discussed fully in 8.5.

8.2.3 Changing column names

8.2.3.1 The default column names

Unless you specify otherwise, the columns in a VIEW 'inherit' the same names as the columns in the corresponding base tables. In other words, they behave exactly as 'normal' result tables. So, if you create a view with:

```
CREATE VIEW eastsales AS
        SELECT empno,surname FROM salesmen
            WHERE region = 'East';
```

then the view called 'eastsales' will have two columns, called 'empno' and 'surname'.

```
Empno Surname
-------------
10001 Smith
20002 Brown
```

8.2.3.2 How to change column names

You can specify different column names as an optional part of CREATE VIEW. Simply include a comma-separated column name list after the name of the view. The list must be contained in brackets, and it must contain headings for *all* the columns in the SELECT clause.

The columns selected by the SELECT statement will be assigned to your 'alternative' column names on a 'left to right' basis. For example:

```
CREATE VIEW eastsales (Employee,Name,HalfYear) AS
        SELECT empno,surname,q1target+q2target
    FROM salesmen
        WHERE region = 'East';
```

will give a view with three columns

```
Employee    Name        HalfYear
--------------------------------------
10001       Smith          78000
20002       Brown         145000
```

In any subsequent operations on the data in the view, you must refer to those columns by their new names. So,

```
SELECT empno FROM eastsales;              ** ILLEGAL **
```

has to be discarded in favour of:

```
SELECT employee FROM eastsales;
```

8.2.3.3 When you have to specify different column names
There are three situations when you *must* define specific column names for
the view. These are:

- when the view is created with columns of the same name from more
  than one base table.
- when one of the columns is a calculated column or contains an
  aggregate function.
- when one of the columns contains a non-ANSI-SQL function.

In all these cases, SQL cannot decide by itself what to call the view
columns. You have to set up the names yourself. Here are three examples:

1.
```
CREATE VIEW twotables (Employee,surname,empnum,amount) AS
    SELECT s.empno,s.surname,c.empno,c.amount
    FROM salesmen s, contracts c,
    WHERE s.empno = c.empno;
```

where a column called 'empno' is picked up from both base tables.

2.
```
CREATE VIEW eastsales (empno,surname,halfyear) AS
    SELECT empno,surname,q1target+q2target
    FROM salesmen
    WHERE region = 'East';
```

where the calculation 'q1target+q2target' has to be assigned a name.

3.
```
CREATE VIEW eastsales (empno,surname,YearJoined) AS
    SELECT empno,surname,YEAR(datejoined)
    FROM salesmen
    WHERE region = 'East';
```

This example uses the dBASE IV function 'YEAR()' to display only the
year from the date. Of course, this type of function is not in the ANSI
standard, but you will find that every implementation contains useful
functions similar to this.

8.2.4 The WITH CHECK OPTION

8.2.4.1 What does WITH CHECK OPTION do?
The WITH CHECK OPTION clause is used to ensure that whenever a view
is updated with INSERT or UPDATE, no values are allowed to be entered
which contravene the 'formula' which CREATEd the view. In other words,

you can only enter into a view rows which satisfy the condition used to create the view. Let us illustrate this with an example:

```
CREATE VIEW largetargets AS
        SELECT empno,surname,q1target FROM salesmen
        WHERE q1target > 150000;
```

If the WITH CHECK OPTION clause is not specified, then it would be perfectly possible to INSERT a row for a salesman whose target is only 30000:

```
INSERT INTO eastsales VALUES
        ('40004',
        Marks,
        10000);
```

The 'salesmen' base table will, quite correctly, be updated to include this row. However, the row will immediately disappear from the view, since it does not satisfy the view formula of 'WHERE q1target > 150000'.

Although this behaviour is logical, it seems to go against the whole idea of having the view in the first place. If a user is supposed to be seeing only salesmen with targets over 150000, then he should not really be allowed to update the base table with targets of values under 150000.

The problem can be avoided if you use the WITH CHECK OPTION clause. If we created 'largetargets' as:

```
CREATE VIEW largetargets AS
        SELECT empno,surname,q1target FROM salesmen
        WHERE q1target > 150000
        WITH CHECK OPTION
```

then the INSERT statement above will be rejected, as it should be.

8.2.4.2 *Restriction on WITH CHECK OPTION*

You can only use WITH CHECK OPTION on a view which is updatable. See section 8.5 for a full discussion of which sorts of views are allowed to be updated. If you attempt to specify WITH CHECK OPTION on a non-updatable view, then the whole CREATE VIEW command will fail.

You would usually want to specify the WITH CHECK OPTION clause on any (updatable) view that you create.

8.2.4.3 *Using WITH CHECK OPTION to validate data entry*

As you can see, WITH CHECK OPTION provides a useful way to validate data entry into base tables. The only 'validation' checks otherwise provided by ANSI SQL are the CREATE TABLE options NOT NULL and UNIQUE.

If you want to ensure that Quarter 1 target figures are *never* entered as zero or less than zero, then you could define a view:

```
CREATE VIEW salesentry AS
      SELECT * FROM salesmen
            WHERE q1target > 0
      WITH CHECK OPTION;
```

If all data entry to the base table 'salesmen' is carried out through the identical view 'salesentry', then no targets of zero or less will be allowed through.

8.3 Deleting a view – DROP VIEW

ANSI SQL makes no provision for removing a view from the database – just as it makes none for removing a table! However, the de facto standard command for deleting a view is:

```
DROP VIEW viewname;
```

This is used in exactly the same way as the DROP TABLE command. For example:

```
DROP VIEW eastsales;
```

will remove the view definition for 'eastsales' from the appropriate System Catalog tables.

Any other views dependent on the dropped view (i.e. those which reference the dropped view in their own CREATE VIEW definition) will also be dropped from the database.

8.4 Using views

Once a view has been created, you can carry out on the view most of the operations that you can carry out on base tables. (The exceptions to this rule are given in section 8.5.) The most common action, of course, will be to query the view with SELECT.

If we create 'eastsales' as:

```
CREATE VIEW eastsales AS
      SELECT empno,surname,q1target
      FROM salesmen
            WHERE region = 'East'
```

(showing all salesmen in East Region)

we can then *query* it with commands like:

```
SELECT * FROM eastsales;

SELECT surname,qltarget FROM eastsales;

SELECT empno,qltarget FROM eastsales
    WHERE qltarget > 200000;
```

We could *update* it with commands like:

```
INSERT INTO eastsales VALUES
    (30003,
     'Adams',
     95000);
```

You can even use a view in the SELECT clause used to *create another view*. You could say:

```
CREATE VIEW nextview AS
    SELECT empno,surname FROM eastsales
        WHERE surname LIKE 'S%';
```

to create a view showing all salesmen in East Region whose surname begins with 'S'.

8.5 Restrictions on views

There are two types of restrictions on what you can do with views. They are:

— restrictions on the SELECT statement used to create the view in the first place
— restrictions on what you can do with a view once it has been created

As always, the different SQL implementations have slightly different rules about what is and is not allowed when creating and using views. However, since the rules are, in the main, based on what it is logically possible to achieve with a view, this is one of the areas where most SQLs are fairly consistently in agreement.

   As an example of a logically impossible operation, consider a view based on the GROUP BY statement (the view itself is perfecly valid):

```
CREATE VIEW regiontotals (Region,Total) AS
    SELECT region,sum(qltarget) FROM salesmen
        GROUP BY region;
```

This would produce a view showing something like:

```
Region      Total
---------------
South       500000
West        600000
North       250000
East        450000
```

You could *not* issue a command such as:

```
INSERT INTO regiontotals VALUES        ** ILLEGAL **
     (Southwest,
     500000);
```

There is no way that this statement can be related to anything in the underlying base table – it is logically impossible. All SQL implementations would reject such a command on a grouped view.

In the next sections, we will cover all the restrictions on views in some detail.

8.5.1 Restrictions on SELECT when CREAT(E)ing a VIEW

In the SELECT statement used to create a view:

– you may not use UNION
– you may not use ORDER BY

It is perfectly acceptable to use ORDER BY and UNION when querying an existing view. So, although you could not say:

```
CREATE VIEW eastsales AS
     SELECT empno,surname FROM salesmen
     WHERE region = 'East'
     ORDER BY empno;               ** ILLEGAL **
```

you can get the result that you want by first creating the view as

```
CREATE VIEW eastsales AS
     SELECT empno,surname FROM salesmen
     WHERE region = 'East'
```

and then querying it with:

```
SELECT * FROM eastsales
     ORDER BY empno;
```

Similarly, you could not say:

```
CREATE VIEW eastwestsales AS          ** ILLEGAL **
        SELECT empno,surname FROM salesmen
              WHERE region = 'East'
  UNION
            SELECT empno,surname FROM salesmen
                  WHERE region = 'West';
```

But you could get the same result by creating two views for East Sales and West Sales regions, and then combining them in a SELECT:

```
SELECT * FROM eastsales
UNION
SELECT * FROM westsales;
```

Of course, in this particular example you would have been better off using an 'IN list' or an 'OR' condition in the original SELECT used to create the view.

```
CREATE VIEW eastwestsales AS
        SELECT empno,surname FROM salesmen
              WHERE region IN ('East','West');
```

8.5.2 Restrictions on using existing views

Most of the restrictions on using existing views affect the commands for updating tables – INSERT VALUES and UPDATE. However, grouped views (those created with a GROUP BY clause), and views created using functions or calculations, are also subject to certain restrictions on SELECT. There are rules governing what can and cannot be done with existing views; these are summarised in 8.5.2.1.

As we mentioned in section 8.5, what you can and cannot do with a view depends on what is logically possible. To help you to understand the operations that *are* logically possible, here is an explanation of how SQL interprets commands on views.

SQL commands acting on base tables act directly on the 'real' data in the base rows. A command issued on a VIEW does not have any 'real' data directly available to work on; the formula of the view is 'getting in the way' of the base table. When SQL sees a command issued on a view, it uses the view 'formula' to reformulate that command as if the command had been made on the base table. If such a reformulation does not produce a valid SQL statement, then the command is rejected.

8.5.2.1 Rules for creating updatable views

In ANSI SQL, a view is only updatable if all the conditions below apply to the view definition (that is, to the SELECT expression that defines the view).

1. It does not include the DISTINCT option
2. It does not include a function or a calculation
3. The FROM clause references only one table (which itself must be updatable)
4. The WHERE clause does not contain a subquery
5. There is no GROUP BY clause
6. There is no HAVING clause

And of course, we have already said that CREATE VIEW does not support the ORDER BY or UNION clauses in the SELECT definition.

8.5.2.2 Examples of updatable views

For example, if 'eastsales' has been created as

```
CREATE VIEW eastsales AS
      SELECT empno,surname,q1target FROM salesmen
            WHERE region = 'East';
```

then an UPDATE statement such as:

```
UPDATE eastsales
      SET q1target = q1target *1.1;
```

(to increase everybody's targets by 10%)

will be reformulated internally by SQL as:

```
UPDATE salesmen
      SET q1target = q1target*1.1
      WHERE region = 'East';
```

This, of course, is a perfectly valid SQL statement. 'Eastsales' is therefore said to be an *updatable* view.

8.5.2.3 Examples of non-updatable views

However, if 'regiontotals' had been created as a view containing an aggregate function and a GROUP BY clause, such as:

```
CREATE VIEW regiontotals (region,total) AS
      SELECT region,SUM(q1target) FROM salesmen
      GROUP BY region;
```

then a command such as

```
        INSERT INTO regiontotals VALUES        ** ILLEGAL **
            ('Southwest',99000);
```

will be reformulated as something like:

```
        INSERT INTO salesmen (region,SUM(qltarget)) VALUES
            ('Southwest',99000);                ** ILLEGAL **
```

This is not a valid SQL statement, since you cannot specify a column containing an aggregate function in an INSERT command. In addition, the 'Southwest' region has no obvious relationship with anything in the 'salesmen' table – it does not contain salesmen's employee numbers or individual targets etc. The view violates rules 2 and 5 of the list we gave in 8.5.2.1.

Here is another example of a non-updatable view. This time, the view contains data from more than one table, thus violating rule 3 from the list above. If the view was created as:

```
        CREATE VIEW twotables AS
            SELECT s.empno,s,surname,c.amount
                FROM salesmen s, contracts c
                WHERE s.empno=c.empno;
```

then the update attempt:

```
        INSERT INTO twotables VALUES
            ('40004',
             'Spencer',
             39000);                            ** ILLEGAL **
```

will fail. SQL cannot reformulate the statement into anything resembling a valid INSERT command, since INSERT cannot reference two tables at once.

Of course, you could argue that SQL should be enhanced to *give* it the capabilities to translate such a command into the two separate INSERT VALUES statements that would be required to perform the update successfully. After all, the human eye can easily see that what the update is intended to do is add one row to 'salesmen' (entering employee number 40004, called Spencer), and also add one row to 'contracts' (entering employee number 40004's contract amount of 39000). However, SQL is not capable of performing such translations in its current state.

8.5.2.4 *Rules for querying views*
As we saw in 8.5.2.1, the rules for permitting updates on views are fairly well defined. However, it is not so easy to define precisely what restrictions

there are on SELECTing from views. Perhaps the best that we can do is to state the obvious and say that *when the query is 'reformulated', it* **must** *form a valid SQL statement.*

There are some general guidelines that can be laid down:

1. A view column derived from an aggregate function or calculation may only be named in the SELECT or ORDER BY clauses of the SELECT statement used to query the view.
2. A view column derived from an aggregate function may not itself be used with a function.
3. A view created from a GROUP BY clause cannot be joined with another table or view.
4. A view created from a GROUP BY clause cannot use a WHERE, GROUP BY or HAVING clause in a FROM statement.

8.5.2.5 Examples of non-queryable views
Here is an example of another illegal command attempted against the grouped view 'regiontotals' defined in 8.5.2.3. In this case, we are attempting to SELECT all regions where the 'total' figure is greater than 500000.

```
SELECT region,total FROM regiontotals        ** ILLEGAL **
            WHERE total > 500000;
```

This will be reformulated by SQL as:

```
SELECT region,SUM(qltarget) FROM salesmen    ** ILLEGAL **
            WHERE SUM(qltarget) > 500000
            GROUP BY region;
```

This is not a valid SQL statement, since WHERE clauses cannot contain aggregate functions. It violates rule 1 in 8.5.2.1.

Below is an example of a violation of rule 2 in our list. This produces a 'nested' function in the reformulation, which is not permitted in SQL. If we perform the following query on 'regiontotals':

```
SELECT AVG(total) FROM regiontotals;         ** ILLEGAL **
```

then SQL reformulates it as something like:

```
SELECT AVG(SUM(qltarget)) FROM salesmen;     ** ILLEGAL **
```

8.5.2.6 Why restrictions on views are a problem
Views present a confused interface to the SQL user. In many situations they function exactly as base tables do, allowing users to query and update data freely. In other situations, the fact that a view is an 'extraction' of data

from other tables prevents the user from carrying out what at first glance appear to be identical operations. When you consider that in many cases users of an SQL application will not be aware that they are using a view rather than a base table, it is hardly surprising that users are sometimes irritated to find that, so far as they are concerned, an 'identical' command works fine on one table but not another.

On the other hand, as we have seen, there are good reasons why apparently 'valid' commands *have to* fail on some views. SQL implementations have yet to work out a consistent way of informing the user of the reasons which cause failures in view access and updates; however, there *must* be something better than Informix's ubiquitious 'Invalid SQL statement' message!

8.6 Using views to preserve perceived data structures

You can see from the previous sections that views can be used both to save users' time when performing frequent identical operations on the database, and to restrict the data items a user is allowed to access.

Views are also a useful way of preserving the same user interface to data through changes to the underlying table structures. In any production application, existing table structures often have to be changed, either because the database design was not correct in the first place, or because changes in the business have made necessary the addition or deletion of columns and tables. Whatever the reason, such changes can be very confusing for the average user.

For example, the database manager may decide that, owing to the company's new requirement to break down salesman's targets over different product lines for analysis, it will now be more sensible to 'split' the 'salesmen' table into two. One table will hold the salesman's name, address, date of birth etc; the other will hold multiple rows for each salesman, showing the quarterly targets for each product. Some users will need to know about this change in order to access the new information available. But if the majority of users simply need to continue to see the salesman's employee number, name, and total targets per quarter, then the database manager could create a view to 'reproduce' the data originally held in the old 'salesmen' table.

The view could even be given the name 'salesmen' (provided of course that the new tables were created with different names!). Those users not affected by the new requirement would never even be aware that the database structure had changed.

Summary

In this chapter you saw how SQL lets you create and delete views which provide different perspectives on the database. Views are useful because:

1. They save users time in entering complex SELECTs.
2. They are an easy way to restrict the data that a particular user is allowed to access.
3. They can be used to 'cushion' users against changes in underlying database structures.

We also looked at some of the restrictions on creating and using views.

9 *Optimising performance*

Overview

This chapter deals with ways of improving the performance of an SQL database. We will talk about options available in every SQL implementation, such as indexing, and changing the design of queries.

Major commands and topics covered

CREATE INDEX   Query design
DROP INDEX

9.1 Introduction

If you understand all the commands that we have covered so far in this book, then you will certainly be able to get SQL to do more or less anything you want it to do, from creating tables and views, through inputting data, to SELECTing any set of data that you need. But it may not do it as quickly as you would like!

You will find that there are several ways by which you may be able to speed up SQL. Some are things which all SQLs support. Others are specific to a particular implementation. Here we will cover in some detail the options available to all SQL users, and give a brief rundown on some of the implementation-specific ones. None is essential to the correct operation of an SQL system; on the other hand, they may make the difference between users being happy to use the computer or deciding that it would be quicker to use pen and paper instead!

9.2 Indexing a table – CREATE INDEX

9.2.1 *What is an index?*

An index provides SQL with a quick way to 'look up' entries in a table (just as an index to a book provides a quick way to look up topics in the text). An index groups all identical entries for a particular column (or columns) together, letting SQL access those entries almost instantaneously.

SQL uses indexes for two, totally unrelated, purposes. The primary use for an index is to speed up data access. The second thing most SQLs use an index for (contrary to the principles of the relational model) is to enforce uniqueness of rows. The UNIQUEness concept and SQL's misuse of it is covered in section 4.4.5.2. We will talk about the use of the CREATE UNIQUE INDEX command in section 9.2.2.3.

Note for dBASE III and IV users

Users of **dBASE III and IV** (not dBASE IV SQL) and some other PC-based non-relational databases have a 'definition' problem with the word 'index'. In dBASE, one of the primary uses of an index is to order the data. In SQL, the index has *no effect whatever* upon the sequence in which rows are displayed; this is controlled solely by the ORDER BY clause in a WHERE condition.

9.2.2 *Using CREATE INDEX*

9.2.2.1 *The basic command*
You set up an index with the CREATE INDEX command. The syntax of this is:

```
CREATE (UNIQUE) INDEX indexname ON tablename
    columnlist
```

For example, to set up an index on the contracts table to speed up access by employee number, we would say:

```
CREATE INDEX contempno ON contracts
    (empno);
```

The column on which the index is created is called the **index key**.

This now provides 'quick access' to the values in the 'empno' column. For example, a query such as:

```
SELECT empno,amount FROM contracts
    WHERE empno = '10001';
```

would execute much more quickly.

9.2.2.2 Indexes on multiple columns (concatenated indexes)
If you need to access data based on more than one column of a table, you can specify several columns in the index key. For example:

```
CREATE INDEX empcust ON contracts
    (empno,custname);
```

This would speed up a query such as:

```
SELECT empno,custname,amount FROM contracts
    WHERE empno = '10001'
    AND custname = 'Brown Brothers';
```

This kind of index is also called a **concatenated index**.

9.2.2.3 The UNIQUE option
Most SQLs use the UNIQUE option on CREATE INDEX as their only way of enforcing that a table does not contain duplicate rows. (Whether or not this is the best way of achieving that result is discussed in section 4.4.5.3). A UNIQUE index created on the primary key of the table will ensure that no 'doubling up' of data can occur. For example, in the 'salesmen' table, there should only ever be one entry for any one employee number. If no index, or an index without the UNIQUE option, exists on the 'empno' column, then most SQLs would be quite happy to let you have multiple entries for the same employee number. You could issue the command:

```
INSERT INTO salesmen (empno,surname) VALUES
    ('10001', 'Smith');
```

followed by

```
INSERT INTO salesmen (empno,surname) VALUES
    ('10001', 'Brown');
```

and end up with *two* entries under employee number 10001.
   However, if an index was created by:

```
CREATE UNIQUE INDEX ON salesmen
    (empno);
```

then the attempt to insert a second entry for '10001' would be rejected.
   The UNIQUE option can apply equally well to indexes which have multiple-column keys. The command:

```
CREATE UNIQUE INDEX empcustdate ON contracts
        (empno,custname,contdate);
```

would enforce the contracts table's primary key of the combination of employee number, customer name, and contract date.

9.2.3 What does an index look like?

You can think of an index as a separate file containing pointers to the original table. Conceptually, it looks rather like this:

```
Original Table                    Index on 'empno'
-------------                     ---------------


Empno    Amount
---------------
20002    10,000                        10001
10001    25,000                        10001
30003    15,000                        20002
90009    50,000                        20002
20002    25,000                        30003
10001    13,000                        90009
```

To help you see how the index works, we have drawn lines between the first two index entries and their corresponding rows in the base table.

Details of indexes (i.e. the table that they were created on, and the key used to create them) are stored in one of the System Catalog tables. You can see what indexes are available for a table with a SELECT command like:

```
SELECT * FROM sysidxs
      WHERE tbname = 'contracts';
```

(this uses the dBASE IV SQL catalog table 'sysidxs').

The index is not itself a table, and you cannot access it with commands like SELECT, UPDATE etc. Indeed, you cannot access it directly at all! All you can do with an index is CREATE it or DROP it. It is SQL that decides whether or not to use an index to help with a retrieval command; it is SQL that updates the indexes as changes are made to the table.

9.2.4 How does it speed up data access?

To show how using an index can speed up the system, consider the 'contracts' table in our example database. Let us assume that it has five thousand entries, only two of which are for employee number '10001'. If the table has no index associated with it, then a query such as:

```
SELECT * FROM contracts
    WHERE empno = '10001';
```

(to see all the contracts for employee number 10001), has to examine every row in the table to see whether it refers to this employee.

However, if an index has been created on the employee number column, then SQL can go immediately to the first entry for employee 10001. It then passes rows to the result table until it reaches a row for employee 10002. At this point it 'knows' that there are no more entries for 10001, so it stops looking through the base table.

Since there are only two entries for employee 10001, SQL has only had to examine two rows instead of five thousand. Obviously, it is impossible to quantify the actual time saved by using the index, since that depends entirely on the computer system used. However, we can certainly say that the operation *with* the index will be much faster than without.

9.2.5 Index overheads

From the above example, you might assume that it would be a good idea to create indexes on every possible column and combination of columns, just to cover the remote possibility that you might need them some day! However, this would not be sensible.

Maintaining an index makes extra work for SQL. After every change to the database (every INSERT, UPDATE or DELETE), SQL has to check which indexes are affected, and record the new data. This all takes time. Updating one index takes a small amount of time (probably insignificant); updating twenty indexes might take so long that the user starts to complain about the response time of the system. In addition, indexes take up space on the disk. This may or may not be a consideration for you; however, in principle you do not want to waste resources unnecessarily.

Indexes also take time to set up in the first place. It may well be worth spending five minutes creating an index on 'empno' if you know that you are going to be doing frequent queries based on employee numbers. If you are doing a 'one off' enquiry to find all employees whose address contains the postcode 'W1', then you would be better off just performing the query, and not wasting time setting up the index at all.

9.2.6 When does SQL use indexes?

9.2.6.1 The 'general' rule
We mentioned above that the user has no control over whether or not an index is used by SQL for any particular operation. SQL looks at the

command that it has to process and the available indexes, and 'decides' which, if any, index to use. The SQL module which controls this process is called the **optimiser**. The optimiser's job is to examine a query, and decide upon the most efficient strategy for producing a result. The more 'intelligent' the optimiser, the better the performance of the SQL system will be. The 'rules' followed by any optimiser will probably change in different releases of any SQL product, since the SQL suppliers are naturally always working on increasing the efficiency of their products.

Different SQL implementations have slightly different internal 'rules' about index usage. However, it is possible to generalise about usage so that you can decide whether or not it is worth setting up an index on a particular column.

The basic rule for index use is that if:

– there is a WHERE clause in the statement being parsed.

and

– at least the first column mentioned in the WHERE condition (for any particular table) has had an index created on it

then

– SQL will definitely use the index.

9.2.6.2 Examples of using/not using an index

So, if an index has been created on the employee number of the 'contracts' table, then the following commands will *certainly* use the index:

```
SELECT * FROM contracts
      WHERE empno = '10001';


SELECT * FROM salesmen,contracts
      WHERE salesmen.empno = contracts.empno;
```

The next command will *definitely not* use the index, since the WHERE clause does not reference the 'empno' column at all:

```
SELECT * FROM contracts
      WHERE custname = 'Brown Brothers';
```

In the example in the next command, where 'empno' is referenced as the second column in the WHERE clause, the situation is less clear cut. Here we move into the realms of the differences between SQL implementations; some might use the existing index, others might not.

```
SELECT * FROM contracts
      WHERE custname = 'Brown Brothers'
      AND empno = '10001';
```

9.3 Rephrasing commands to force index use

9.3.1 Why should you rephrase commands?

Notice that you could easily rephrase the WHERE condition in the section above to make sure that SQL *does* use the index. Simply reversing the order of the clauses will give:

```
SELECT * FROM contracts
      WHERE empno = '10001'
      AND custname = 'Brown Brothers';
```

There are many situations like this where you can control whether an index is used or not.

By now, you should have realised that SQL has a high level of **redundancy** in its SELECT command. You can often achieve an identical result by combining different operators in different ways. Sometimes, one method will yield the result significantly more quickly than others.

For 'one off' queries, it probably really does not matter which form of SELECT you use. Use whichever is easiest for you to understand! But for frequently-used retrievals, you should try to find the quickest method available – the one that will use an index.

Here are a few situations to avoid when setting up queries. In all the following situations, SQL will be unable to use an index to speed up processing. In many cases, you could rewrite the query to allow an index to be used.

This list is certainly not exhaustive. Nor is it the case that these 'rules' will work in all SQL implementations (or even, for that matter, in future releases of DB2). The best advice that we can give regarding 'speeding up' your system is that, if a query seems to take an inordinately long time, consider whether it could be rephrased to achieve the same result, and try it out!

9.3.2 Examples of conditions that will not use indexes

(The examples here are taken from DB2.)

9.3.2.1 Using NOT with LIKE, BETWEEN, IN, EXISTS

SQL does not use an index if the WHERE clause depends on a NOT operator. So if an index had been set up on the 'amount' column on the contracts table, then:

```
SELECT * FROM contracts
      WHERE amount BETWEEN 10000 AND 34000;
```

will use the index, whereas

```
SELECT * FROM contracts
        WHERE amount NOT BETWEEN 10000 AND 34000;
```

will not use the index.

Solution
Rewrite the query to use < and >, or an **IN(list)**. So:

```
SELECT * FROM contracts
        WHERE amount >= 10000
        AND amount <=30000;
```

will use the index.

9.3.2.2 *Comparing a column with a column or literal of a different length*
SQL will not use an index if the items being compared are of different lengths. For example, let us say that two tables contain a field 'surname', and table1 defines it as CHAR(**15**) whereas table2 has defined it as CHAR(**20**). Even if table2 has an index set up on 'surname', then the following SELECT could not use it.

```
SELECT table1.surname, table2.amount FROM table1,table2
        WHERE table1.surname = table2.surname;
```

Similarly, if a column is to be compared with a constant, then the constant must be of the same length. For example, if the 'empno' column is defined as being CHAR(**5**), then a SELECT to extract all entries from 'contracts' for employee number 10001 will not use the index if the constant is defined as a 6-character item:

```
SELECT *  FROM contracts
        WHERE empno = '10001 ';
```

9.3.2.3 *Using a concatenated index in the 'wrong' order*
If you have set up a concatenated index, then in some situations keys other than the first will not be used. For example, if you set up an index on 'salesmen';

```
CREATE INDEX regemp ON salesmen (region,empno);
```

the index will be used in the two follwing queries (where **region** is referenced first in the WHERE clause):

```
SELECT * FROM salesmen              (uses both keys)
        WHERE region = 'East'
        AND empno = '10002';
```

```
SELECT * FROM salesmen (uses region key only)
     WHERE region = 'East'
     AND qltarget = 50000;
```

But the index will not be used in a query such as:

```
SELECT * FROM salesmen
     WHERE empno = '10001';
```

or in a join like:

```
SELECT * FROM salesmen,contracts
     WHERE salesmen.empno = contracts.empno;
```

because in these two queries there is no mention of the **region** key.

Solution
If you are going to reference the employee number in this way frequently, then you should set up another index which has 'empno' as the first or only column in the index key.

9.3.2.4 Calculations on index key columns
If the WHERE clause includes a calculation on a column which has had an index created on it, then the index will not be used. For example, if we have set up an index on 'q1target', then the query:

```
SELECT * FROM salesmen
     WHERE qltarget = 60000;
```

will use the index. But the following queries will not:

```
SELECT * FROM salesmen
     WHERE qltarget * 4 = 240000;
```

and

```
SELECT * FROM salesmen
     WHERE qltarget + q2target = 200000;
```

9.3.2.5 Character strings beginning with a 'wild card' (%)
Indexes cannot be used on character strings beginning with the 'any character' sign '%'. So this query on the indexed column 'empno' :

```
SELECT * FROM salesmen
     WHERE empno = '%0001';
```

(to find any employee number ending in '001'), will not use the index.

Solution

This can be difficult to avoid. But you may be able to use an 'IN(list)' instead. For example, if you are really only interested in employees 10001, 20001, 50001 and 70001, you could say:

```
SELECT * FROM salesmen
        WHERE empno IN ('10001','20001','50001','70001');
```

and benefit from the index.

9.4 Deleting an index – DROP INDEX

If you no longer need an index, then you can remove it from the database with the DROP INDEX command. You simply say:

```
DROP INDEX indexname;
```

For example, to get rid of the 'regemp' index created in 9.3.2.3, you would say:

```
DROP INDEX regemp;
```

9.5 Add-on products to help you to design efficient queries

Most suppliers provide some help for users attempting to unravel the complexities of the most efficient way to write queries. In fact, most suppliers devote a few pages to this subject in the system documentation, which will probably be enough to point you in the right direction for your particular implementation. Users of the more established SQL systems often have available 'add-on' products – such as System Center's 'DB/ Optimize' for DB2 users – which can be set to examine any query and suggest ways in which it might be made more efficient. As SQL systems become more widespread in the PC marketplace, we can expect that such 'add-on' products will become available for a wider range of systems.

9.6 Other ways of improving performance

Improving query design is not the only way to improve performance. Most SQL systems have various 'parameters' – for example, space allocated to the various system areas – which can be changed to optimise the performance of your particular needs on your particular computer system. In addition, most suppliers provide utilities to assign tables, indexes, etc to particular physical storage areas which correspond to the 'logical' storage requirements of the database. This should help to group together tables which are frequently accessed together. We are not going to deal with these techniques here – they are implementation dependent, and have no relation to the SQL language itself. But remember that reorganisation of the physical and logical storage of your databases can often lead to performance gains.

Summary

Now you know how to improve the performance of your SQL system by using – or choosing not to use – indexes. You are also aware that you may be able to improve performance by juggling the way that your SQL implementation stores the databases. And last, but by no means least, you know that it is worth looking for 'outside help' in the form of add-on products which may help you to pinpoint weak points in your querying techniques.

10 Database security and integrity

Overview

This chapter deals with the problems of keeping the data in the database intact.

Major commands and topics covered

GRANT
REVOKE

10.1 Introduction

It is obviously important for any system that stores potentially confidential information to be able to control *who* is allowed to access *what*. It is also important that, once a user has established his right to access and update a particular data item, the system should be able to control *what data* is entered.

The first type of control is known as **database security**. The second type is called **database integrity**.

In fact, we have already covered in previous chapters the measures that can be taken to preserve database integrity. We will summarise them briefly in section 10.3 just to remind you.

The major part of this chapter will deal with database security measures.

10.2 Database security

10.2.1 Who controls database security?

Up to this point in the book we have been looking at SQL as though we were using it on a 'single user' system. We have made no provision for checking whether, having learned the UPDATE command, a user is actually allowed to use it! But in practice, the majority of installed SQL systems are running on multi-user systems. Somebody, with the aid of the SQL GRANT command, has to be in charge of allocating **authorisations** and **privileges** to all the users of the SQL database. This person is usually known as the Database Administrator (DBA). If you are using SQL on a single-user microcomputer system, *you* will be the DBA. Obviously, your job in this case will not be very demanding! If you are an 'ordinary' user on a multi-user system, you may never get the chance yourself to use the DBA-level commands that you will learn about here. However, even 'ordinary' users can use the security commands to some extent (for example, to control other people's access to their own tables); and even a 'single-user' DBA may find it useful to set up different user names to prevent him from abusing his own powers by mistake! So all users of an SQL system need to know about the security controls that SQL can provide.

10.2.2 Overview of SQL's security levels

SQL provides a very flexible way of controlling access to data. Access is controlled at two different levels.

Level 1 – authorisation to use the SQL system, with password protection on entry to the system.

Level 2 – privileges assigned to a particular user, applicable at table level.

At the 'highest' level, a user is GRANTed an 'overall' access level to the system. GRANTing authorisation is also sometimes known as 'enrolling' a user onto the system. When a user is enrolled onto the SQL system he is assigned:

– a user name
– a password, (or 'identifier')
– an authorisation level which controls the general type of operation that he is allowed to carry out on the database

Most SQL systems demand that the user should 'log in' to the database by providing his user name and password. SQL checks these entries in the appropriate System Catalog table, and 'looks up' the authorisation level belonging to this user.

Once in the SQL system, GRANT can control the type of operation that each user can carry out on a particular table or view. The privilege levels available range from SELECT (query capability only) through to UPDATE, and can apply to a whole table or to selected columns.

The privilege levels assigned to a user for a particular table take priority over the user's general authorisation level. So a user whose authorisation level in principle allows him to UPDATE any table in the database may find that his privilege level for the 'salesmen' table only allows him to SELECT data.

The combination of authorisation and privileges gives the DBA very tight control over who can do what to the database.

We will discuss the authorisation and privilege levels in detail in the following sections.

10.2.3 *Differences between SQL implementations*

Most SQLs provide the dual-level security system described briefly above. But, naturally, the different SQLs enforce slightly different authorisation and privilege options. You may find that your particular SQL does not, for example, have a privilege level called 'INDEX', or that your implementation's CONNECT authorisation allows users to do more (or less) than the option described here. Here, we will use the Oracle options for illustration purposes. However, the principles of allocating correct access controls remain the same regardless of the exact options available.

You will also find that, while privileges are always allocated by GRANT, the method for assigning authorisations varies considerably between implementations. Oracle uses a version of the GRANT command; DB2 and Informix assign authorisations when a database or schema is created; and dBASE IV SQL does not implement authorisations at all!

Note for dBASE IV SQL users
dBASE IV SQL is unusual in that there is no 'forced' log-in to the system , and so there is no authorisation level of security. You can choose to run dBASE with PROTECT set on, in which case a log-in sequence will be demanded; however, this has no relation to SQL's authorisation procedures.

10.2.4 *Ownership of tables and views*

Up until now we have made the tacit assumption that all table operations we have learned (SELECT, UPDATE, DELETE etc) are being carried out by the creator of that table. We have therefore not needed to specify the owner of the table as part of the table name. However, once we introduce the concept of a multi-user database, it becomes vitally important to know who created a table. Users have complete freedom of usage over tables that they themselves have created; however, they have *no* rights to do anything with tables created by other users, unless such rights (or 'privileges') are GRANTed to them. Table names may always be prefixed by the user name allocated when a user is enrolled into the SQL database. So, if the 'salesmen' table was created by user 'david', we could validly say:

```
SELECT * FROM david.salesmen;
```

The USER associated with a table is stored in the System Catalog as part of the table definition. If you give a command which does not prefix the table name with a user name, then SQL assumes that you are referring to a table that *you* created. For the sake of clarity, we will refer to tables by their 'full' names throughout this chapter.

10.2.5 GRANT and REVOKE

GRANT and REVOKE are the two SQL commands concerned with controlling which users have access to the SQL system, and at what privilege level. The same command is used for both authorisation and privilege level allocation.

GRANT is used to give users authorisations and privileges; REVOKE is used to remove a previously GRANTed authorisation. (In fact, ANSI SQL does not support REVOKE. However, since it is another of the 'obviously useful' commands which DB2 *does* support, you will find it available in most SQL implementations. Oracle, Informix and dBASE IV SQL all use it.)

10.2.6 GRANT for authorisations

10.2.6.1 The syntax of GRANT
The form of the GRANT command to enrol a new user or to change the status of an existing user, is:

```
GRANT authorisation level TO username
      IDENTIFIED BY password;
```

For example:

```
GRANT CONNECT TO liz
      IDENTIFIED BY pword;
```

Once this command has been given, 'liz' can enter the SQL system when she gives the password 'pword'. User names must be unique. However, two users could have the same password.

The levels of authorisation available are (in increasing order of 'powerfulness'):

1. CONNECT
2. RESOURCE
3. DBA

A user can be granted more than one of these authorisations in a single GRANT command:

```
GRANT RESOURCE,DBA TO liz
     IDENTIFIED BY pword;
```

Contrary to what you might suppose, GRANTing DBA authorisation does not automatically confer RESOURCE authorisation as well, although granting RESOURCE does confer CONNECT.

10.2.6.2 What does CONNECT authorisation entitle you to do?

A user with CONNECT authorisation can:

- SELECT from other users' tables
- UPDATE, INSERT and DELETE data from other users' tables

He cannot:

- CREATE his own tables
- DROP other people's tables

10.2.6.3 What does RESOURCE authorisation enable you to do?

Users with RESOURCE authorisation can do everything the user with CONNECT authorisation can do and, in addition:

- CREATE their own tables
- DROP their own tables

10.2.6.4 What does DBA authorisation enable you to do?

A user with DBA authorisation can carry out any operation on any tables in the database. Obviously, the number of users at DBA level should be severely limited!

10.2.6.5 Changing passwords

Once a user has been enrolled, any further reference to that user name will be interpreted by SQL as a change to the user details rather than an attempt to enrol another user. The password can be changed by reissuing the original GRANT command with a new password attached. So:

```
GRANT RESOURCE TO liz
     IDENTIFIED BY newpass;
```

10.2.6.6 Changing authorisations – adding and REVOK(E)ing

New authorisations can be added simply by reissuing a GRANT command. Thus, if 'liz' already has RESOURCE privilege, then DBA privilege could be assigned as well simply by saying:

```
GRANT RESOURCE,DBA TO liz
     IDENTIFIED BY newpass;
```

To remove an authorisation, use the REVOKE command. So to remove the DBA privilege from 'liz', say:

```
REVOKE DBA FROM liz;
```

To remove more than one privilege, list them separated by commas. Thus:

```
REVOKE RESOURCE,DBA FROM liz;
```

You can remove a user from the database completely by REVOK(E)ing the CONNECT privilege:

```
REVOKE CONNECT FROM liz;
```

This last command would remove user liz from the system. However, tables, indexes and views that she created whilst owner of RESOURCE are *not* dropped from the system. Users who have been granted privileges to use those tables can continue to do so, and if 'liz' is reinstated she can access those tables again.

10.2.7 GRANT

10.2.7.1 The syntax of GRANT
The GRANT command for assigning privileges has the syntax:

```
GRANT (ALL/privilege list) ON tablename
     TO user name (PUBLIC)
     (WITH GRANT OPTION);
```

For example, to give user 'liz' the right to UPDATE 'david's table called 'managers', we would say:

```
GRANT UPDATE ON david.managers
     TO liz;
```

If *all* users are to be allowed to access this table, then the PUBLIC option should be specified. So:

```
GRANT UPDATE ON david.managers
     TO PUBLIC;
```

will allow everyone to update david's 'managers' table.
    PUBLIC includes all current and future users of the system.

10.2.7.2 Privilege levels available
The privilege levels supported by ANSI SQL are:

```
SELECT
UPDATE (column list)
INSERT
DELETE
```

In addition, DB2 and many other implementations support the ALTER and INDEX privileges. (ANSI SQL obviously cannot offer an ALTER privilege, since it does not support the ALTER TABLE command!)

Any or all of these privileges can be granted to any user. To grant more than one privilege, separate them by commas; to grant all privileges, you can use the shorthand 'ALL'. It does not matter in what order you specify the privileges. Here are two examples of privileges being GRANTed:

```
GRANT SELECT,UPDATE ON david.managers
     TO liz;
```

and

```
GRANT ALL ON david.managers
     TO liz;
```

You can also assign a set of privileges to more than one user at a time. For example,

```
GRANT SELECT,UPDATE ON david.managers
     TO liz,paul;
```

The names of the privilege levels are self explanatory. Just in case you are not clear about what each level entitles the user to do, here is a brief explanation of each one.

SELECT   Allows the user to perform any retrieval operation with the SELECT command.
INSERT   Allows the user to INSERT new rows into the table.
DELETE   Allows the user to DELETE rows from the table.
ALTER   Allows the user to use the ALTER TABLE command.
UPDATE   Allows the user to UPDATE data in the table.
INDEX   Allows the user to CREATE and DROP INDEXes on the table.

The UPDATE privilege can be selectively applied to a column list. So 'liz' could be given UPDATE privilege on only columns 'address' and 'phone' of the 'managers' table with:

```
GRANT UPDATE (address,phone) ON david.managers
     TO liz;
```

10.2.7.3 Who is allowed to assign privileges?
There are three classes of people who, in different circumstances, can grant privileges to other users to use tables.

Firstly, anyone with DBA privilege can assign privileges to any user for any table.

Secondly, the *owner* of a table (i.e. the person who created it) can assign any privilege level to any other user.

Thirdly, if a user has been assigned the right to access a table WITH GRANT OPTION, then he too can assign other users the same or 'lesser' privileges over the table. A user cannot assign privileges that he himself does not have. So, if 'liz' CREATEs a TABLE called 'salesmen', she can assign 'david' SELECT, INSERT and UPDATE privileges on that table with:

```
GRANT SELECT,INSERT,DELETE ON liz.salesmen
      TO david
      WITH GRANT OPTION;
```

The user 'david' can then himself GRANT any other user the right to SELECT, INSERT or DELETE from the salesmen table. For example, he could say:

```
GRANT SELECT ON liz.salesmen
      TO paul;
```

But if he tried to GRANT a privilege which he does not himself have, such as UPDATE, then the GRANT to 'paul' will fail.

He can also 'pass on' the WITH GRANT OPTION if he wishes. So 'david' could have said:

```
GRANT SELECT ON liz.salesmen
      TO paul
      WITH GRANT OPTION;
```

which will allow 'paul' to GRANT the SELECT privilege on 'salesmen' to yet another user.

10.2.8 Removing privileges – REVOKE

REVOKE is used to remove a privilege from a user. Anyone with DBA authorisation can REVOKE privileges from any user; owners of a table can revoke privileges from anyone to whom they have previously GRANTed a privilege. You can REVOKE any or all of the user's privileges. For example,

```
REVOKE DELETE ON liz.salesmen
     FROM david;
```

will remove david's ability to DELETE the table, although he will still be able to use his INSERT and SELECT privileges.

```
REVOKE ALL ON liz.salesmen
     FROM david;
```

will remove his right to access that table at all.

10.2.9 Cascading REVOKES

When a user REVOKEs a privilege that he previously GRANTed to another user, that privilege is automatically removed 'all down the line'. In other words, if user 1 GRANTs a privilege to user 2 WITH GRANT OPTION, and user 2 GRANTs it to user 3, then when user 1 REVOKEs the privilege from user 2, user 3 will lose it as well. In this way, REVOKEs can 'cascade' down a line of users, reaching people the originator of the REVOKE never intended to influence.

There is no real way of avoiding this situation. Users simply have to be warned of the danger of REVOK(E)ing a privilege without being sure who will be affected.

10.2.10 Privileges and views

Privileges can be assigned to views in exactly the same way as they can to tables. 'Updatable' views (see chapter 8) can be assigned all privilege levels; 'non-updatable' views can only have SELECT or INDEX allocated. If you attempt to GRANT UPDATE, INSERT or DELETE privilege to a non-updatable view, you will get an error message.

10.3 Database integrity

As we mentioned at the beginning of this chapter, the security measures discussed above are only one aspect of the whole problem of ensuring that the data in the SQL database is correct. There are also various types of integrity constraints which can be applied to data in tables. All these have been covered as separate topics in other chapters of this book. We will summarise them here, together with references to the chapter in which they appear.

At the simplest 'integrity' level, columns are defined as being of a particular data type and width, and may make use of the NOT NULL option (chapter 4). Columns may also be described as UNIQUE (either through the CREATE TABLE command or with a CREATE UNIQUE INDEX statement), which ensures that data is not duplicated incorrectly (chapters 4 and 9). And you can create VIEWS with the WITH CHECK OPTION clause to force base table updates to observe range constraints (see chapter 8).

Another aspect of preserving the integrity of the system is the COMMIT and ROLLBACK commands, which allow easy recovery from mistakes entered into the database (see chapter 7).

You should also look at chapter 13 for a discussion of where ANSI SQL fails to provide adequate integrity constraints.

Summary

This chapter dealt with the security commands that you can use to controls access to the system, to individual tables, and even to specific columns. We also reminded you about the integrity measures that can be used to validate data entry.

11 Embedded SQL

Using SQL statements within a programming language

Overview

This chapter takes a brief look at embedding SQL commands within a host language. It is intended to introduce you to the concepts involved rather than to provide full coverage of the subject.

Major commands covered

SELECT..INTO..	FETCH cursor
DECLARE CURSOR	CLOSE cursor
OPEN cursor	UPDATE..WHERE CURRENT OF
	DELETE..WHERE CURRENT OF

11.1 What is embedded SQL?

So far, we have dealt exclusively with interactive SQL – commands that you type in yourself at the keyboard. Interactive SQL commands are carried out as soon as you enter the semi-colon (;) to indicate the end of a statement.

However, you can also embed SQL commands within standard procedural programming languages, such as C, BASIC, Cobol, and Fortran. Such languages are called **host languages**. There are several variations on interactive commands which can only be used when embedded in a host language.

This book does not attempt to teach you everything about how to use embedded SQL. However, we will give a short overview of the ideas involved, and a list of the 'embedding' commands that are normally used.

In a host language/SQL program, it is the host language which is the 'driving force' in the system. The host is used to write menus, do screen design, output reports – in short, to do all the things that you would normally use a procedural programming language for. The host needs SQL 'merely' as a way of extracting data from the database (of course, this is still the reason for the program's existence in the first place!). Once it has the data, then it is the host's responsibilty to display it, include it in further processing, print it out, or whatever is required. But it is SQL that has to 'bend' itself to work with the host language, rather than the other way around. SQL has to pass data to the host in terms that the host can understand.

Procedural programming languages are not 'set oriented', as SQL is. They prefer dealing with records, and indeed, individual fields, one at a time. Most of the extra commands that SQL employs to interface with the host language are concerned with 'breaking down' the output from an interactive SQL command into a set of **variables** which can be passed to the host language.

dBASE IV has been used for the examples of program code shown here. We have deliberately kept the host language programs extremely simple, since the aim of this section is to show you the new SQL commands, not to confuse you with another language!

11.2 The SQL 'embedded' commands

11.2.1 Host language requirements

11.2.1.1 Variable names
The names of the variables used for passing over data in a form that the host can use must conform to any naming conventions of the host language. In addition, depending on the host used, variables may or may not have to be defined in the host program before the SQL statement is reached.

11.2.1.2 EXEC SQL..
Most host languages expect any SQL statement to be preceded by the command:

```
EXEC SQL
```

For example:

```
EXEC SQL SELECT SUM(q1target) INTO mtotal;
```

This is a 'signal' to the Host/SQL system that the next statement has to be 'translated' into the host language when the program is compiled.

dBASE IV is unusual in that it does *not* require the EXEC SQL statement when SQL is called from a dBASE IV program. However, the EXEC SQL is required if dBASE IV SQL is embedded within, for example, C.

11.2.2 Standard SQL commands embedded in the host program

This is yet another of the areas where different SQL implementations can vary widely. In general, you can use any SQL 'interactive' command embedded in a host language, and it will produce exactly the same result as when you use it 'interactively'. However, some SQLs will not allow you to embed the data definition commands (CREATE TABLE etc).

So you could quite validly give the command within a host language program:

```
DELETE FROM salesmen WHERE empno = '10001';
```

However, when you are using the data manipulation commands (SELECT, UPDATE, DELETE etc) in a program, you often want to access a single row and apply a host language command to that row only. For example, you may want to display the information from one row as a 'form', or to ask the user whether or not this particular row should be deleted. In such cases, you need to use the special SQL commands intended for just this purpose. These commands are described in the following sections.

11.2.3 SELECT..INTO..(variable list)

For example:

```
SELECT surname,qltarget FROM salesmen
      WHERE empno = '10001'
      INTO msurname,mqltarget';
```

This command is used when you expect the SELECT to return a single row. The column values in the result table are assigned to the variables on a left-to-right basis. If more than one row is returned, SQL will just use the first row.

This is the kind of embedded SQL command which might be used if the host language had produced a program to:

– ask the user which employee number he wanted to view
– display the surname and region of the employee

The program would look something like this:

```
ACCEPT 'Which employee do you want? ' TO mempno

SELECT surname,region
       INTO msurname,mregion
       FROM salesmen
       WHERE empno = mempno;

? 'The surname is ' + msurname
? 'The Sales Region is ' + mregion
```

11.2.4 Using CURSORs

If the result of a SELECT is expected to produce more than one row, then you cannot use the SELECT..INTO statement. You have to set up an **SQL cursor**. This is like a pointer which moves through the SELECTed set of rows, passing the values of each row into memory variables. The initial DECLARE CURSOR statement defines a SELECT statement, and the 'result table' produced by that SELECT statement can then be 'stepped through' by various cursor control commands. There are four SQL statements concerning setup and movement of cursors. They are:

```
DECLARE cursorname CURSOR
OPEN cursorname
FETCH cursorname
CLOSE cursorname
```

They are used as follows:

11.2.4.1 DECLARE CURSOR
Syntax:

```
DECLARE cursorname CURSOR FOR
       SELECT statement;
```

This command defines the SELECT statement which will later be executed (by the OPEN command). A cursor must be DECLAREd before it can be referenced in any other cursor-related command. To set up a cursor to retrieve all rows for salesmen in East Region, we could say in the host program:

```
DECLARE eastsales CURSOR FOR
       SELECT empno,surname,qltarget
              FROM salesmen
              WHERE region = 'East';
```

DECLARE statements would normally be placed at the beginning of a program, together with other host language definition statements (e.g. variable declarations)

11.2.4.2 OPEN
Syntax:

```
OPEN cursorname;
```

OPEN is used to execute the SELECT statement defined by the DECLARE CURSOR. The cursor is 'pointed' at the position before the first row of the result table.

To perform the SELECT in the 'eastsales' cursor, we would say:

```
OPEN eastsales;
```

11.2.4.3 FETCH
Syntax:

```
FETCH cursorname INTO memory variable list;
```

The FETCH statement advances the cursor 'pointer' to the next row in the result table. It then passes the column values in that row into a set of memory variables (exactly as the SELECT..INTO.. command does).

To pass the values in the first row of the result table produced by the 'OPEN eastsales' command to a variable list, we would say:

```
FETCH eastsales INTO mempno,msurname,mqltarget;
```

Once the values have reached the variables, then the host language can do whatever it wants with them (display, perform further calculations, print, etc).

Obviously, the FETCH command needs to be enclosed in a loop of some sort. In our dBASE IV program, we could say:

```
DO WHILE .T.
   IF sqlcode = 0
      FETCH eastsales INTO mempno,msurname,mqltarget;
      ? 'Employee '+ mempno+ 'is called' + msurname
   ELSE
      EXIT
   ENDIF
ENDDO
```

We will end up with a list of employee details, one underneath the other.

SQLCODE is a special variable maintained by SQL to check on the result of an embedded SELECT (or FETCH) statement. If SQLCODE is zero, then the result table (or the current FETCH) has values in it, and the program can continue. If SQLCODE is negative, something has gone seriously wrong with the query (for example, querying a table which does not exist). If it is positive, then SQL is issuing a 'warning' (for example, there may be no rows in the result table). A 'real' program (as opposed to the simple examples that we are using here) should make provision for all three cases.

In our example, when the cursor has processed the last row in the result table then SQLCODE will be set to a negative value, and the program will 'EXIT' (jump to the next command after ENDDO).

11.2.4.4 CLOSE
Syntax:

```
CLOSE cursorname;
```

The CLOSE statement releases the memory variables used by the cursor. As a matter of good programming practice, cursors should be CLOSEd when they are no longer required. This is often done at the end of the host language program.

Our example could issue the:

```
CLOSE eastsales;
```

statement immediately after the ENDDO in the loop above.

11.2.4.5 The program listing
Here is the entire program that we put together above:

```
DECLARE eastsales CURSOR FOR
        SELECT empno,surname,qltarget
             FROM salesmen
             WHERE region = 'East';

OPEN eastsales;

DO WHILE .T.
   IF sqlcode = 0
      FETCH eastsales INTO mempno,msurname,mqltarget;
               ? 'Employee '+ mempno+ 'is called' + msurname
   ELSE
          EXIT
       ENDIF
 ENDDO

    CLOSE eastsales;
```

11.2.5 UPDATE and DELETE with cursors

Syntax:

```
UPDATE table SET column = expression
      WHERE CURRENT OF cursor;
```

and

```
DELETE FROM table
      WHERE CURRENT OF cursor;
```

Both of these commands apply themselves to the row that the cursor is currently pointing at.

If you want to check with the user whether a particular row should be updated or deleted, or if you have already used the cursor to point at a row and want to carry out subsequent update or delete, you should use the 'cursor' form of the UPDATE and DELETE commands. These are used in combination with the DECLARE CURSOR, OPEN and CLOSE commands, just as FETCH is. In fact, they are usually used after a FETCH, since the reason for using the 'embedded' form of the command is that you want to access that row individually for some other reason.

For example, if you want to delete a row after checking with the user, you might write the following code:

```
DECLARE eastsales CURSOR FOR
      SELECT empno,surname FROM salesmen
            WHERE region = 'East';
OPEN eastsales;
DO WHILE .T.
  IF sqlcode = 0
      FETCH eastsales INTO mempno,msurname;
      ACCEPT 'Delete employee ' + mempno TO mdel
      IF mdel = 'Y'
            DELETE FROM salesmen
            WHERE CURRENT OF eastsales;
      ENDIF
ELSE
      EXIT
ENDDO
CLOSE eastsales;
```

If you wanted to UPDATE the Quarter 1 target figure instead of deleting the row, then you could replace the DELETE FROM..WHERE CURRENT OF.. with:

```
UPDATE salesmen
SET qltarget = qltarget*2
WHERE CURRENT OF eastsales;
```

Summary

You learned here how to embed SQL commands within a host language. We looked at the special forms of the data manipulation commands, and saw that you can also use the 'interactive' commands within programs.

12   Non-standard SQL

Overview

This chapter looks at those features such as form and report generators which, while not part of the SQL language, are nevertheless very important to users.

It also covers some of the non-ANSI SQL commands available in the four SQL implementations that this book uses, and provides a comparison chart of features available in those four SQLs.

12.1 The user interface – introduction to Oracle

The rest of this book has dealt with the 'core' SQL commands and shown some of the aspects in which four actual SQL implementations differ from the ANSI standard. However, for many users the 'accuracy' of an implementation is a far less important issue than that of its ease of use. Although users want the power of SQL, most of them do not want the hard work of learning the intricacies of the SELECT statement! In practice, users are much more interested in the non-SQL facilities provided by most SQL suppliers – the user interface, the form and menu generators, the report writers, and the interfaces with other industry-standard packages.

Nowadays, nearly all SQLs come with easy-to-use, menu-driven user interfaces, and contain tools to distance the user from the hard-core SQL commands. Although every manufacturer implements its version of these tools in different ways, the basic concept is the same in every system.

In this chapter, we look briefly at the set of tools offered with Professional Oracle. These are representative of the kind of utilities that you would expect to find in any modern SQL implementation.

Naturally, this book is not the place to attempt a full description of all the Oracle facilities; nor is this an Oracle tutorial. All we do here is to show you the kind of add-on features available in most SQL implementations to make the user's life easier.

Oracle – a modular system

The various components of an Oracle system can be bought or installed as separate modules. The only essential part of the system is SQL*Plus – the module which allows you to use SQL statements interactively. Some of the other modules available are:

- SQL*Forms   (a form generator)
- SQL*ReportWriter   (a report writer)
- SQL*Menu   (menu-interface generator)
- SQL*Calc   (spreadsheet)
- Add-In for 1–2–3   (Oracle via Lotus 1–2–3)
- SQL*Graph   (graphs)
- Pro*C   (the C language for Oracle)

The user has to log in to each module separately. For example, to set up a simple application, the developer would first have to use SQL*Plus to create tables; then SQL*Forms to design input and query forms; then SQL*ReportWriter to design printed output; and lastly SQL*Menu to tie all the other elements together.

In other SQL implementations you may find all these elements available within a single 'package'.

In this chapter we will look in some detail at SQL*Forms and SQL*Report-Writer, with a brief discussion of SQL*Menu and the Database Add-In for 1–2–3. SQL*Calc is simply a 1–2–3 like spreadsheet (which can also access data from the Oracle database), and SQL*Graph is a way to extract numeric data from the Oracle database and display it in a variety of graph formats.

12.2 Forms generation – SQL*Forms

12.2.1 What is a forms generator?

A forms generator allows you to develop forms-based applications for entering, querying, updating and deleting data.

First you have to create the form; once it exists you can choose the action you want to use it for (e.g. adding data, or finding records which satisfy particular criteria). Oracle uses function keys to select actions; other SQL implementations use a menu-based control structure.

Oracle's menu-driven form-generator system makes it easy to create both simple and complex forms.

12.2.2 Creating a simple form

Before you can use SQL*Forms, you must have already created a table under the SQL*Plus module of Oracle (the 'area' of Oracle within which you have access to the complete range of SQL commands covered in this book). Once the table or tables have been specified, you can move to SQL*Forms to build the forms that you need.

At the most basic level, the forms generator can automatically produce a form which simply puts the column names (as defined by the CREATE TABLE command) on the screen and allows the user to enter or edit data. All you need to do to achieve this is to tell Oracle:

- what name you want to give to the form
- which table (or tables) you want to work with
- how many rows of data are to be shown on the screen at one time

Oracle will then display its default layout for the form, using the column names and widths already stored in the data dictionary. If the total field widths will fit onto an 80-character screen, then Oracle will choose a 'line based' layout. If the total width is over 80 characters, then Oracle will go for a 'page based' design. Thus the default layout for the 'salesmen' table would be page based, like this:

```
----------------------------------------------------

          --------- Salesmen ---------


          SURNAME
          FIRSTNAME
          EMPNO
          DATEJOINED
          ADDRESS
          PHONE
          REGION
          Q1TARGET
          Q2TARGET
          Q3TARGET
          Q4TARGET


----------------------------------------------------
```

The layout for the 'contracts' table would be line-based:

```
---------------------------------------------------------
              -------- Salesmen --------


     EMPNO   CONTNUM   CONTDATE   CUSTNUM   AMOUNT



---------------------------------------------------------
```

You can choose to display forms from more than one table on the screen at the same time, although to link them together so that the information they display is 'synchronised' – for example, so that a header showing the salesman's name is followed by a list of all the contracts for that particular salesman – you have to embed an Oracle 'macro' or SQL statement (see 12.2.4).

When you use the form for entering data, you can use the cursor keys to move within a row, and to move from one row to the next or previous one. You can also use the 'editing' keys to insert or delete characters and words.

If you chose to show more than one row on the screen, then Oracle will simply move you to the next line when you have finished with the first record. Oracle will automatically validate your entries against the data type of the column. So, if you tried to enter a letter in the AMOUNT field, you would be given the error message 'Legal characters are 0–9'.

12.2.3 Customising the form – Screen Painter and menus

Although the default form is quick and easy to create, most users will want something which looks better on the screen, and which offers more control over input. Oracle provides pop-up menus which give you control of each individual field, allowing you to specify things like:

- whether updates are permitted
- what format the data should appear in
- whether data should be forced into upper case
- default values
- upper and lower range limits
- help messages

The Screen Painter allows you to change text on the screen and 'Cut and Paste' text and fields into different places. You can also improve the look of the form by drawing graphics boxes and lines in appropriate places.

After a few minutes of work, the 'salesmen' form could look like this:

```
--------------------------------------------------------
                    Personnel System
                    ----------------


            Employee Details - Salesmen
            =============================


        Employee Number:            Surname:
        Region:                     First Name:

        Address:                    Joined on:


        ------------------------------------------------
                    Target Details

        Quarter One:                Quarter Two:
        Quarter Three:              Quarter Four:


    --------------------------------------------------------
```

12.2.4 Customising the form – including SQL statements

Oracle allows you to make the validation capabilities of the form as complex as you require by letting you embed SQL statements within the form. These statements can be 'triggered' either when the cursor *enters* a field, when it *leaves* a field, or when a field is *changed*. For example, you could ensure that a valid region code was entered by using the SQL WHERE clause,

```
WHERE :region IN ('N','S','E','W')
```

to be triggered whenever the user changes the contents of the 'region' field.

You can specify help messages to appear when the trigger statement fails. For example, if the user entered a region of 'X', the message:

```
'Valid regions are N,S,E and W'
```

could be shown.

You can use these advanced facilities to do things like:

– generate sequential employee numbers
– verify data by looking up in tables or lists
– look up and display data from other tables
– perform calculations
– synchronise display of data from two tables

12.2.5 Using the form

Once the form has been created, it can be used for:

- adding new rows
- editing existing rows
- deleting rows

To find a particular row to edit or delete, you can specify 'search' criteria simply by entering appropriate data into fields while in 'query' mode. Oracle finds the first record to satisfy your criteria; you can then page forward to see if any more records have been selected.

12.3 Creating reports – SQL*ReportWriter

12.3.1 What is a report writer?

The forms generator discussed above is used for input, and for screen-based access of data. For printed output, a Report Writer can be used to show data in a variety of different formats.

Reports can range from a simple 'tabular' listing, to mailing labels and personalised 'form letters'.

As with forms generation, you first have to create the report layout, and can then use it to display or print the data. Oracle allows you to execute reports either from within SQL*ReportWriter or from the operating system level.

12.3.2 Creating a simple report

SQL*Forms allows you to create a usable form even if you have no knowledge of SQL commands. However, to use SQL*ReportWriter you need to be able to use the SELECT statement in order to tell Oracle:

- which columns are to be included in the report
- which rows are to be shown

This SELECT statement is called the **query** associated with the report. Any valid SELECT statement may be used. For example, to show the names and phone numbers of all salesmen in West Region, you could specify the SQL statement:

```
SELECT surname,firstname,phone FROM salesmen
    WHERE region = 'W'
    ORDER BY surname;
```

To get Oracle to produce a simple tabular report all you have to do is specify:

- the name that you want to give to the report
- the name that you want to give to the query
- the query statement itself

The report can have more than one query associated with it.

Oracle will take default values from the data dictionary for items such as column widths, column headings and display formats.

The simple report produced by the above SQL statement would look like:

```
            -- SALESMEN DETAILS --
Surname         Firstname           Phone
-------         ---------           -----

Smith           John                01-123-4567
Jones           Jane                0435-54896
```

12.3.3 Customising the report

The default report is unlikely to look good enough for most users' purposes. Oracle provides easy-to-use menu options to allow you to do things like:

- change the column headings
- add a page header and footer
- group the rows (e.g. by region)
- add a group header and footer
- change the display format for a column
- summarise data (using any of the SQL aggregate functions)
- link data from different tables (e.g. to show all contracts for each salesman)
- produce calculated fields

It is also easy to produce a report which is page based rather than tabular. For example, you could easily produce a report which showed the data for each record in exactly the same layout that we used for the screen-based form in 12.2.3.

A variation on this technique can be used to produce personalised 'form letters'. The report format for such a letter would look something like:

Dear Mr &SURNAME,

We are pleased to confirm our offer of a job as Salesman. You will be working for &REGION region, and your target for the third quarter 1990 will be &Q3TARGET.

We look forward to you joining us on &DATEJOINED.

12.4 Creating a menu interface – SQL*Menu

12.4.1 What is a menu interface?

A menu interface (or menu tree) is a series of interconnected menus from which users can select and perform certain tasks. Using a menu tree makes it easy for end-users to use the computer system effectively with minimal knowledge of SQL.

SQL*Menu allows developers to set up quickly an easy-to-use system from which users can do things like:

- enter and query data using forms created in SQL*Forms
- run reports created in SQL*ReportWriter
- run graphs created in SQL*Graph
- execute SQL*Plus command files

Setting up the menu tree simply involves:

- assigning a name to each menu
- setting up the text for each menu option
- assigning a command to be carried out when a menu option is selected

Special features include:

- controlling user access by allowing different groups of users to access different options from the menus
- setting up help screens

12.5 Oracle Database Add-In for Lotus 1–2–3

It can be useful for users of both Oracle and Lotus 1–2–3 to be able to query data from the Oracle database and feed results directly into a Lotus 1–2–3 spreadsheet.

Once the Database Add-In has been installed, an SQL statement can be embedded into a spreadsheet simply by entering it into a worksheet cell preceded by the special function '@SQL'. For example, you could access the total Quarter 1 target for all salesmen by moving to cell A1 and entering the command:

```
@SQL(SELECT SUM(q1target) FROM salesmen;)
```

The contents of this cell can be used in other 1–2–3 formulae in exactly the same way as a 'normal' worksheet cell. For example, to see the effect of a

10% increase in the Quarter 1 target figures, you could go to cell B1 and enter the formula:

```
+A1*1.1
```

Users familiar with SQL can enter the SQL statements directly; however, Oracle provides a help system (compatible with 1–2–3's familiar menu and help structures) allowing users to 'build' valid SQL statements step by step.

12.6 Differences from ANSI SQL in DB2, dBASE IV SQL, Informix and Oracle

In the first part of this chapter we looked at the kind of utilities which make the task of using SQL much easier, although they themselves are certainly not part of the SQL language. However, as you will have gathered from previous chapters, most SQL implementations also contain 'deviations' from ANSI SQL which *are* considered to be part of that particular set of SQL commands. Here we will take a brief look at some of the more important commands available in the 'core' set of statements of the four SQL implementations that we have used throughout the book.

All these SQLs have available lots of 'interactive' commands which are not part of the 'core' ANSI/DB2 SQL command set. Here are a few of the most obvious areas where such commands make the product easier to use (although quite possibly less 'relational'!). We have mentioned the major commands for each product in each area to make it easier for you to track them down in the manuals. This is certainly not an exhaustive list, but it will give you an idea of the kind of features that you might expect to find in a 'typical' SQL product.

12.6.1 *Formatting column displays*

You may want to show dates in different formats, or display numbers to different numbers of decimal places.

Check out:

DB2	–	Query Management Facility (QMF)
dBASE	–	SET DATE, SET FORMAT
Oracle	–	COLUMN..FORMAT, SET NUMFORMAT
Informix	–	FORMAT COLUMN

12.6.2 Improving the display of a result table

Result tables show the information you want, but often in a very repetitive fashion. Without resorting to full-fledged report generation utilities, you can get an improved SELECT display (especially in the area of showing subtotals and totals) with commands such as:

```
DB2        -   Query Management Facility
                              (QMF)
Oracle   -  BREAK, COMPUTE
Informix  -  FORMAT
```

dBASE IV SQL does not offer any such commands in this area.

12.6.3 Improving ease of access to System Catalog data

Although all the data about everything in the database is held in the System Catalog, it can be long-winded to perform common tasks such as looking at the column names for a particular table. In addition, it can be helpful to add descriptions to tables and columns so that users can see what they are for! Taking this even further, DB2 has an EXPLAIN command which shows the strategy that SQL adopts when processing any data manipulation commands (SELECT, UPDATE etc). This can be very useful when you attempt to optimise queries.

Check out:

```
DB2        -      COMMENT ON, EXPLAIN
Oracle   -      COMMENT ON
                     DESCRIBE table
dBASE    -      SHOW DATABASE
Informix  -      DESCRIBE DATABASE/TABLE
```

12.6.4 Using functions to manipulate part of a column

All our four SQLs provide a wide range of functions, ranging from 'conversions' (for example, character to number, date to character), through 'strings' (for example, upper to lower case and vice versa, and accessing only part of a field), through 'arithmetic' (for example, absolute values, modulus), and many more.

12.7 Chart comparing main features in the four SQL implementations

This chart shows some of the major areas where these four SQLs differ, or at least, might be expected to differ. Remember that they all offer a fairly complete SQL implementation, supporting most if not all of the ANSI standard commands. We have not included ANSI standard features which they *all* support, since this would not be particularly informative. As you know, they all allow you to create tables and views, update and delete data, and perform complex SELECTs on tables. (There is at least one 'SQL' product – not one of our four – which does not even support the CREATE TABLE command!)

Feature Comparison Chart

Feature	DB2	dBASE	Informix	Oracle
Table and column structures – Maximums				
Column width (chars)	254	254	32,767	240
Columns per row	300	255	U/L	255
Row size (bytes)	32,714	4000	32,767	U/L
Size of numeric fields (digits)	15	36	32	40
Length of index key (bytes)	255	100	U/L	U/L
No.columns in index	16	U/L	U/L	U/L
No. of columns in ORDER BY		U/L	8	15
Total length of all ORDER BY columns	4044 bytes	100 bytes	U/L	U/L
Security				
Passwords on entry to SQL database	Yes	No	No	Yes
Include INDEX privilege as well as all ANSI privileges	Yes	Yes	Yes	Yes
Table definitions				
NULLs supported	Yes	No	Yes	Yes
Data types in addition to ANSI standard	Date Graphic Time	Date Logical Serial	Date Money	Date Raw Long RowID

Functions

Aggregate functions in addition to ANSI standard	None	None	None	STD VAR
Date functions	Yes	Yes	Yes	Yes
Time functions	Yes	No	Yes	Yes
Arithmetic functions	Yes	Yes	Yes	Yes
Financial functions	No	Yes	Yes	Yes
Trigonometric	No	Yes	No	Yes

NON-ANSI commands

ALTER TABLE	Yes	Yes	Yes	Yes
DROP xx	Yes	Yes	Yes	Yes
REVOKE	Yes	Yes	Yes	Yes

WHERE clause

Outer join	No	No	Yes	Yes
UNION	Yes	Yes	Yes	Yes
INTERSECT	No	No	No	Yes
DIFFERENCE	No	No	No	Yes

User Interface

Command driven	Yes	Yes	Yes	Yes
Forms generator	Yes	No	Yes	Yes
Report generator	Yes	No	Yes	Yes
Menu generator	Yes	No	Yes	Yes

Summary

This chapter gave you a feel for the kind of add-on features that you would hope to find in an SQL product. If you are evaluating SQL implementations with a view to buying, then the availability and quality of these 'user-interface' features should certainly form a major part of your evaluation criteria.

It also showed you some of the non-ANSI commands that you might find useful in particular SQL implementations.

13 The relational database model

Overview

In chapter 1, we mentioned that SQL is based on relational principles. This chapter discusses in some detail the relational model as defined by Dr E.F. Codd.

Each of Codd's 12 'Fidelity Rules' is quoted, together with a brief explanation of why that rule is significant for database design, and where (if appropriate) ANSI standard SQL fails to meet the requirements of a relational database system.

You will see that although SQL is a database manipulation language based on relational principles, none of the SQL/RDBMS implementations available today succeeds in faithfully implementing all the 'rules' of the model.

13.1 Introduction

By this point in the book, you should have a fairly good understanding of SQL. You are now in a position to be able to look at the theory which underlies the SQL language.

In chapter 1, we briefly mentioned **the relational model** as being the 'inspiration' for SQL. Now we will discuss that model in more detail.

13.2 Background to relational theory

To claim that a DBMS is 'relational' is, in fact, to make a very precise claim indeed. A relational database should conform to the relational model first described in 1970 by Dr Edgar Codd (at the time working for IBM), and refined upon ever since. In his original paper on the subject (Codd 1970), Codd revolutionised the mainframe and mini world by presenting a radically new way of viewing the data in a database system. Previously, databases were hierarchical or networked; now, a more powerful method of holding and accessing data had been introduced.

It is important to realise that Codd did not produce an implementation of the relational model. In 1970, the relational model was a mathematical model embodying criteria which any implementation would have to meet to be called truly relational; however, the actual translation of the concepts into 'real' systems has been left to the individual software designers. As we said in chapter 1, Codd feels that no existing database systems conform fully to the relational model!

Although Codd remains one of the relational model's greatest exponents, his views do not go unchallenged. There are frequent discussions between experts as to the 'correct' or 'best' way to define various of the relational 'rules'. Indeed, Codd's own ideas about the relational model have matured, not surprisingly, over the past twenty years. The results of these esoteric discussions will no doubt slowly percolate down to the real world of ANSI standards and 'practical' SQL implementations.

In the PC world, the buzz word 'relational database' has come to have the very generalised meaning of 'a database which can access information from more than one file at one time'. Thus in the early 1980s the best selling dBASE II was tagged by its suppliers as 'relational' because it could draw data from two files simultaneously. However, as you will see below, the relational model demands much more of the system than just that!

In 1986 Codd published a set of 12 rules which summarise the criteria that a database system must meet to qualify as relational. These are summarised below; to discuss them in detail would take a whole book by itself. Even IBM's DB2 only 'scored' 7 out of a possible 12; all other systems came even lower.

Of course, a low score on the 'relational test' does not make a product unusable. The popular PC product dBASE IV (not dBASE IV SQL) would probably score 0 in the test; even so, millions of users have produced complex applications using dBASE IV and its predecessors. However, it is certain that the trend is towards developing database systems that conform more fully to the relational model; implementations which do not conform may eventually find themselves out of the mainstream of technology.

13.3 The 12 'Fidelity Rules'

The rules quoted here were defined by Codd in an attempt to clarify the properties a relational database should have (Codd 1986). What we will attempt to do in this section is to explain the practical meaning of each rule, and to talk briefly about whether or not ANSI SQL manages to implement that rule successfully. For further details of the precise meaning of the rules, and areas in which ANSI SQL falls short in various 'minor' ways, you should read the Codd article, or Chris Date (1988). Although Codd's

Fidelity Rules are known as the 'twelve' rules, there are actually thirteen of them! They start with Rule 0.

13.3.1 The foundation rule

Any system claiming to be a relational DBMS must manage the database entirely through its relational capabilities.

All this is saying is that a 'real' relational database system must not mix relational and non-relational features. The 'relational capabilities' referred to are defined precisely in the following 13 rules. As you will see, neither ANSI nor any other SQL satisfies all 13 rules; therefore no current SQL implementation completely satisfies the foundation rule either.

13.3.2. The information rule

All information in a relational database must be represented explicitly at the logical level in exactly one way – in tables.

What does this rule mean?
This rule means what it says – all data, including information about the database itself, must be kept in tables with a row/column structure.

One advantage of tabular structures is that they are:

– *familiar* (the column/row structure of a table is intuitively clear)
– *general* (most types of data can easily be represented in them)
– *flexible* (they can easily be restructured vertically (selecting columns), horizontally (selecting rows), or both ways)

Another advantage is that if all data is stored in tables, and nothing but tables, then the DBMS can apply mathematical operations and strict logic to them. This eliminates many of the deficiencies of 'traditional' database storage methods.

Codd produced a set of fundamental operations on tables, drawn from mathematical set theory, which always result in a new table being derived from one or more other tables.

These operations are known as:

– Selection (retrieving a specified set of rows)
– Projection (retrieving a specified set of columns)
– Product (retrieving all possible combinations of one row from each of two tables)
– Union (retrieving all rows appearing in either or both tables)
– Intersect (retrieving only the rows that appear in both of two specified tables)

- Difference (retrieving all rows that appear in the first, but not the second, of two tables)
- Join (retrieving all possible pairs of rows that jointly satisfy a specified condition)

Although the rule does not directly specify so, any relational database system which keeps all data in tables should be able to support all of these operations.

To what extent does SQL support rule 1?
This is one of the few rules that ANSI SQL, and indeed every current SQL implementation, do support fully. The tabular structure of 'real' relational database systems is seen as the 'trademark' of the relational concept.

13.3.3 Guaranteed access rule

Every data value in a relational database is guaranteed to be logically accessible by resorting to a combination of table name, primary key value, and column name.

What does this mean?
This means that you should be able to 'pick up' any value in any column, provided that you:

- know the name of the table
- can identify the correct row using the *primary key*
- know the column name

To what extent does SQL support rule 2?
Problems can arise here with the primary key concept. In principle, every table should have a primary key – a column or combination of columns whose values uniquely identify a particular row. (In the 'salesmen' table in our example database, the column holding the employee number ('empno') acts as the primary key. There should be no more than one entry for each employee number; therefore the value in 'empno' is enough to distinguish that row from all others.)

However, ANSI SQL does not explicitly support primary keys. As a result, most SQL implementations allow duplicate rows in a table – an idea which is completely contrary to the relational model as defined by Codd. Certainly, it is possible to choose to enforce primary keys by using the UNIQUE option (either with CREATE TABLE or with CREATE UNIQUE INDEX – see chapter 9 for a discussion of this point), but if the user chooses *not* to use primary keys, then he has no way of logically distinguishing one row from another.

So ANSI SQL, and most current SQL implementations, do not enforce support of this rule.

13.3.4 Missing information rule

Missing value indicators (distinct from empty character strings or a string of blank characters, and distinct from zero or any other number) must be represented and supported at the logical level, in a systematic way, independent of data type. The DBMS must support manipulative functions for these indicators which must be independent of the data type of the missing information.

What does this mean?
This rule is talking about **three-way logic**. Any column should show a value as either known and 'positive' (e.g. 'Smith', or 50000, or even -50000), known and 'blank' (e.g. ' ' or 0), or not known (NULL).

In databases not based on the relational model, information is usually stored on a two-way logic basis, and there is no way to tell the difference between a column in which the value has 'intentionally' been left blank (for example, the phone number column when the person does not have a phone), and a column where the value is blank because its value is 'unknown' (for example, the phone number column when we know that the person has a phone, but we do not know the number). In theory, the opportunity to record a third 'logical state' should be a major advantage.

To what extent does SQL support rule 3?
ANSI SQL, and most SQL implementations, offer a limited support for this rule in the shape of the NULL entry. Any column can have the 'value' NULL entered in, to distinguish it from 'known but blank or zero'. For example, you could say:

```
INSERT INTO salesmen (empno,qltarget,phonenumber)
    VALUES ('10001',
             0,
             NULL);
```

NULL can be used for a column of any data type, and any column can be queried with the IS NULL/IS NOT NULL operator. This satisfies the second part of the rule.

However, NULLs are not implemented consistently even within a single implementation. For some commands they are ignored, (e.g. the AVG function); for others they may be included. Codd's associate, Chris Date, has said that given the current state of NULLs in ANSI SQL, it would probably be have been better to leave them out completely! (Date, 1988).

So the rule is supported in theory, but in practice leaves much to be desired.

13.3.5 System Catalog rule

The database description must be represented at the logical level just like ordinary data, so that authorised users can apply the same relational language to its interrogation as they apply to regular data.

What does this mean?
This means that all the details of the tables, views, indexes, etc that make up the database, should be stored in tables just like 'real' data, and should be able to be accessed using exactly the same commands.

To what extent does SQL support rule 4?
ANSI SQL does not support this rule at all! The ANSI standard makes no attempt to define a rule for system catalog design. However, in practice, all 'real' SQL implementations seem to support the rule fully. All SQLs support a System Catalog consisting of tables which the user can access with the SELECT command. For example, the dBASE IV SQL user can say:

```
SELECT * FROM syscols
        WHERE tbname = 'salesmen';
```

and see the column names and descriptions for the salesmen table.

13.3.6 Comprehensive language rule

No matter how many languages and terminal interaction modes are supported (for example, fill-in-the-blanks mode), at least one language must:

-   be expressible as character strings per some well defined syntax
-   be comprehensive in supporting all of:
    1. data definition
    2. view definition
    3. data manipulation (interactively and by program)
    4. integrity constraints
    5. authorisation
    6. transaction boundaries (commit and rollback)

What does this mean?
At least one of the ways of manipulating the database must be a high level language (i.e. not binary, and not purely a 'fill-in-the blanks', easy-to-use

terminal entry capability). That language (in our case, SQL) must allow users to define tables and views, and to retrieve and update data. It must support 'built in' checks on data entry, and allow access to tables and views to be controlled by some kind of password check. It must also recognise that to preserve the integrity of the database, it must be possible to 'undo' transactions (where a transaction may be a single command or a 'logical' group of commands). And it should be possible to 'embed' SQL commands within a 'programming language' (in the broadest sense), or to use them interactively.

To what extent does SQL satisfy rule 5?
In a general sense, ANSI SQL and virtually every other SQL supports this rule. After all, SQL *is* a language expressible as character strings, which can define data and views, etc. That is what this whole book has been about! However, within the various categories, the manner of implementing the requirements varies considerably.

13.3.7 View updatability rule

The DBMS must have a way of determining (at view definition time) whether a view can be used to:

- insert rows
- delete rows
- update which if any of the columns of the underlying base tables

It must store the result of this investigation in the System Catalog.

What does this mean?
In chapter 8 we discussed views in some detail. You know from those discussions that some views are updatable, and some, by the nature of the 'formula' on which they are built, are not. For example, a view which shows just the employee number and region from the 'salesmen' table is updatable; a view showing the grouped total targets for each sales region is not.

The DBMS has to have some way of knowing whether a view is, or is not, updatable.

To what extent does SQL satisfy rule 6?
Since ANSI SQL does not define a System Catalog (see rule 4), it cannot in theory support this rule either.

This is another rule which most 'real' SQLs satisfy reasonably well. Every SQL has a table in the System Catalog which holds VIEW details, including the formula on which the view is based. From this it can determine whether any particular attempted update is permissible.

13.3.8 Set level update rule

The capability of operating on whole tables applies not only to retrieval, but also to insertion, update and deletion of data.

What does this mean?
This means that you should be able to apply any 'data manipulation' operation (SQL's SELECT, UPDATE, INSERT and DELETE) to any part of a table, from the whole table through to one or zero rows. In other words, you should never be constrained to search a table manually row by row to find the record that you require.

To what extent does ANSI SQL satisfy rule 7?
All SQLs offer the ability to scan a whole table for any data manipulation command. For example:

```
UPDATE salesmen
      SET qltarget = 100000;
```

(to give all salesmen a target of 100000), and

```
DELETE FROM salesmen
      WHERE region = 'East';
```

(to scan the whole table and remove everyone in East Region).
   So this rule is in general well supported.

13.3.9 Physical data independence rule

Application programs and interactive terminal activities should not have to be modified when changes are made to internal storage or access methods.

What does this mean?
This means that if, for example, the database is moved from one disk to another, users should remain unaware of the change. No SQL command should depend on knowing physically where data is located.

To what extent does ANSI SQL support this rule?
ANSI SQL, and all other current SQL implementations do support this rule. It is the DBMS itself which notes where data actually resides; all SQL commands simply refer to data items by their logical names.

13.3.10 Logical data independence rule

Application programs and interactive terminal activities should not have to be modified when information-preserving changes of any kind that theoretically permit unimpairment are made to the base tables.

What does this mean?
If tables are split into component parts or renamed, then since all the data in the original components is still there in the new ones it is theoretically possible for data manipulation activities to continue as before. (Of course, if data items (tables, views, columns) are deleted, then some changes to existing queries would have to be made.) So, any relational database language should provide facilities to 'fake' the original data structures so that existing queries can continue to be run.

To what extent does ANSI SQL support rule 9?
Since all SQLs support the concept of VIEWs, they all support this rule. A VIEW with the name of the original table can be created, 'pulling together' the items in the original table from their new logical locations. In theory at least, data manipulation commands should run unchanged.

However, since VIEWs are subject to various 'updatability' constraints (see 8.5), the same queries and updates may not run in practice.

13.3.11 Integrity independence rule

Integrity constraints specific to a particular relational database must be definable in the relational data language, and stored in the System Catalog (not the application programs).

What does this mean?
You should be able to set up 'integrity constraints' – checks on the validity of the data – using SQL, and not be left relying on writing programs to do data validation. SQL should itself keep track of any constraints that you have defined.

To what extent does ANSI SQL satisfy rule 10?
You can certainly set up integrity constraints within SQL, and those that you set up are stored in the System Catalog. However, ANSI SQL is very limited as to the constraints that you can use. Virtually all that you can do is use the CREATE TABLE command to:

-   define columns as NOT NULL
-   define a column as UNIQUE
-   define the data type and width of a column

Another kind of integrity constraint is the VIEW defined with the WITH CHECK OPTION. This allows you to use WHERE conditions to place much tighter constraints on data entry to the base table.

However, it is in principle always possible to bypass a view and enter data directly into the base table, thus bypassing the integrity constraints.

ANSI SQL does not enforce use of primary or foreign keys, which are one of the principal 'integrity' elements of the relational model.

DB2 allows you to specify DEFAULTs (of blanks or zero, as opposed to NULL) as part of a column definition. It would be useful if SQL supported a 'looser' DEFAULT option (allowing the user to define his own defaults for a particular column), and included a RANGE CHECK on a column definition – for example, to ensure that salesmen's targets are never less than zero, or greater than 500000.

13.3.12 Distributed independence rule

Applications programs and interactive terminal activities should not have to be modified when data is distributed or redistributed on different computers.

What does this mean?
This is really a 'wider' version of rule 8. In the same way that users should not need to be aware what area of disk their tables reside on, they should not need to know which computer their tables are on either.

To what extent does ANSI SQL support rule 11?
At the time of writing, such support is not mentioned in the ANSI specification. This whole topic is really 'talking futures' in practical terms; the possibilities of distributing SQL databases over networked computers are only just starting to become reality. IBM has said that DB2 will support this rule at some future date.

13.3.13 Non-subversion rule

If a DBMS has a low level (procedural, one-record-at-a-time) language, that low level cannot be used to subvert or bypass the integrity rules and constraints expressed in the higher level relational language (multiple-records-at-a-time).

What does this mean?
This means that any language controlling access to an RDBMS cannot be allowed to 'cheat' and perform operations that are contrary to the rules of the main data manipulation language. For example, if a column is defined as NOT NULL by the main DML (in our case, of course, SQL), then no

er method of accessing the column should be allowed to enter a NULL value.

other method of accessing the column should be allowed to enter a NULL value.

To what extent does ANSI SQL satisfy rule 12?
The ANSI standard does not attempt to address this rule. ANSI is only responsible for SQL – 'the higher level relational language' mentioned in the rule definition. Any other language used to access the 'database engine' is beyond ANSI's scope.

Summary

As you have seen, the ANSI standard cannot be said to be 'fully relational' by Codd's definition. Nor are any other SQL implementations much better.

However, regardless of how 'relational' SQL really is, it has come to be the language most closely associated with databases based on the relational model. You have to work with what exists, and learn to ignore its shortcomings. There is little doubt that SQL databases will become the standard on microcomputers, minis and mainframes over the next few years. All that users can do is hope that suppliers can agree on a genuine 'standard' SQL, whether or not it fulfils all the demands of the relational model.

Bibliography

American National Standards Institute: Database Language SQL, Document ANSI X3.135–1986

D.Beech: 'New Life for SQL', Datamation, February 1st 1989

E.F. Codd: 'A Relational Model of Data for Large Shared Data Banks'. Communications of the ACM, Vol.13, No. 6 (June 1970)

E.F. Codd: 'The Twelve Rules for Determining how Relational a DBMS product is', The Relational Institute Technical Report, 16/5/86

E.F. Codd: 'Fatal Flaws in SQL', Datamation, August 15th and September 1st 1988

C.J. Date: A Guide to the SQL Standard, Addison-Wesley, 1988

C.J. Date: Where SQL falls short, Datamation, May 1 1987

Appendix A *SQL commands grouped by category*

This table includes all the ANSI SQL commands, plus those non-ANSI commands which are found in most, if not all, SQL implementations (e.g. DROP, ALTER).

COMMAND	*DESCRIPTION*
Data Definition Language:	
ALTER TABLE	Adds columns to an existing table
CREATE DATABASE	Assigns a physical and logical location for a group of tables
CREATE INDEX	Creates an index on a table
CREATE SCHEMA	Assigns a logical location for a group of tables
CREATE TABLE	Creates a table, specifying columns
CREATE SYNONYM	Creates an alternative name for a table or view
CREATE VIEW	Creates a view from one or more base tables
DROP (XX)	Removes a table, index, synonym or view from the database

COMMAND	DESCRIPTION
Data Manipulation Language:	
DELETE	Removes rows from a table
INSERT	Adds new rows to a table
SELECT	Retrieves rows from a table
UPDATE	Changes existing data in a table
Data Control Language	
COMMIT	Stores work permanently in the database
GRANT	Assigns authorisations and privileges
REVOKE	Removes authorisations and privileges
ROLLBACK	Restores database to the state after last COMMIT

Appendix B   Background to the four SQLs

DB2

DB2 was not the first commercial implementation of SQL to come onto the market. However, once it was launched by IBM in 1983 for its MVS mainframe systems, it quickly established itself as the de facto standard for SQL systems. Its close relative for VSE and VM systems, SQL/DS, is very similar to DB2. Many of the commands available in DB2 but not ANSI SQL, such as ALTER and DROP TABLE, have been adopted by other SQLs.

There are various add-on products available for the IBM SQL products, such as System Center's SQL/EDIT and SQL/REPORT (providing the full screen form and report generators that SQL/DS lacks), and DB/OPTIMIZE (to help with the task of interpreting DB2's EXPLAIN output and recommending the best strategies for optimising queries). Informix Software also produce a report generator for DB2 called Report/DB2.

dBASE IV – Version 1.0

When Ashton-Tate launched dBASE IV in 1988, a fully-fledged SQL implementation was included in addition to all the features which dBASE IV added to dBASE III+. This implementation does not include NULLs, which are an important feature of most other SQLs. Nor does it integrate very well (or at all) with most of the features that make dBASE attractive to PC users – the report generator, forms generator, and Control Centre menus. It does, however, allow the user access to all the dBASE functions and SET commands, and SQL commands can be embedded in the dBASE programming language. In addition, SQL tables can be converted to dBASE IV databases.

Given that it is 'thrown in' with dBASE IV, it represents good value for money! Its inclusion with the best-selling dBASE has probably had the effect of introducing the idea of SQL into the PC world much more effectively than any advertising by other suppliers. However, in this

169

version, it is unlikely that many people would buy dBASE just for its SQL facilities.

A new version of SQL is promised with the next release of dBASE IV. As of early 1990, this release had not materialised; nor was Ashton-Tate able to provide a pre-release version for review for this book. If the new version of SQL removes existing bugs, and integrates with the 'user-friendly' features of dBASE IV, then it could become a strong competitor to the other SQL products in the PC marketplace.

Informix-SQL

Informix Software has produced one of the more commonly used SQL systems, available on Unix-based minis and on PCs. In addition, the Informix database engine forms the basis for proprietary SQL products such as the Uniplex database module.

It comes as standard with a simple forms generator ('Perform'), a report generator ('Ace'), a menu tree generator, and a help module which allows naive users to 'build' their database a step at a time. The system operates a 1–2–3 style menu system; alternatively, experienced SQL users can type commands directly.

Also available is Informix-4GL, a fourth generation language which allows users to create full-blown applications quickly and easily. The SQL command set is the same as that of Informix-SQL.

Oracle (Version 5.1.22)

Oracle Corporation produced one of the first commercial SQL implementations (for Unix-based minis), and has since gone from strength to strength. Oracle is now available on IBM mainframes, minis, and PCs. It has a very robust implementation of SQL, similar in many ways to DB2, and generally has a good reputation in SQL circles. It also provides lots of 'extra' commands which can make practical use of the SQL database much easier (for example, outer joins, DIFFERENCE and INTERSECT as well as UNION, the CONNECT clause, no restriction in subqueries on references to the 'main' table, and the ability to CREATE a new TABLE AS a SELECT clause).

The Oracle package includes SQL*Forms, SQL*ReportWriter and SQL*Menu for easy-to-use form based input, report generation, and production of menu-driven applications. It also has an interface to Lotus Corporation's 1–2–3, and has its own spreadsheet, SQL*Calc.

Index